YOUR Magickal YEAR

YOUR
Magickal YEAR

Transform your life through the seasons of the zodiac

Melinda Lee Holm

Illustrations by **Rohan Daniel Eason**

CICO BOOKS
LONDON NEW YORK

For Jamie

Published in 2022 by CICO Books
An imprint of Ryland Peters & Small Ltd

20–21 Jockey's Fields   341 E 116th St
London WC1R 4BW   New York, NY 10029

www.rylandpeters.com

10 9 8 7 6 5 4 3 2 1

Text © Melinda Lee Holm 2022
Design © CICO Books 2022
Illustrations © Rohan Daniel Eason 2022

A CIP catalog record for this book is available from the Library of Congress
and the British Library.

ISBN: 978-1-80065-095-4

Printed in China

Designer: Allan Sommerville
Commissioning editor: Kristine Pidkameny
Senior commissioning editor: Carmel Edmonds
Senior designer: Emily Breen
Art director: Sally Powell
Creative director: Leslie Harrington
Production manager: Gordana Simakovic
Publishing manager: Penny Craig
Publisher: Cindy Richards

Contents

Introduction

Welcome to the first day of the rest of your life. From here on out, things are going to be a little different—and then they'll be a *lot* different. How different and in which ways is all up to you. Some of the changes you make in your life may be visible to all, but the most profound will be visible only to you. That's the thing about personal revolution—it's really about your experience of your life, not about any of the external markers, such as where you live, what you do for work, or who you hang out with. All of these things play their part, but they aren't the star of the show. That role belongs to you alone.

The process I present to you here takes a full year to complete and is intended to be repeated every year, growing with you as you grow. All of the rituals and practices in this book are specific enough to match with particular points of the year, yet flexible enough to allow you to tailor them to fit the circumstances of your life as they change through the years. You can begin at any time, you can take a break and pick back up as needed, but eventually you'll want to return to the rituals and activities you missed along the way. Each one has its own distinctive magickal potential and area of influence that offer opportunities you just can't get anywhere else. Let that be freeing, not stressful. If each new and full moon, every solstice and equinox, offers specific transformational support, that means you don't have to try to change everything about your life at once or wonder what to focus on at any given time. The universe is good like that. If you listen closely, it's a built-in protection from energetic burnout.

As you move through the year, you'll gain knowledge and experience that will be lifelong assets in your personal growth and understanding. Learning to ride the tide of the magickal seasons connects you more deeply with yourself and with the ancient lineage of humans who gazed up at the stars, saw themselves, and started taking notes. The spark of this work has been within you all along. It's time to ignite the flame.

What is a Magickal Year?

The marking of time into years has been accomplished in many ways throughout history. In the Western world, we are currently following a Gregorian calendar year which divides the time it takes the Earth to travel around our Sun into 365 days (plus those pesky leap years). Lunar calendars—which mark the passage of time by the cycles of the Moon—are used to determine the dates of religious holidays in many cultures, particularly throughout Asia. Astrological calendars tell us which planet is in what sign and when. So, what is a magickal year?

A magickal year marks the passage of a year in all of these ways, but more importantly it asks you to focus on how to ride the waves of energy offered by the movement of the planets through the stars to make the most of their magickal potential. Magickal years are more about what you do with the time than how it passes. To follow a magickal year is to make a full lap of the stars, touching on each full and new moon, every solstice and equinox, to honor its influence and open yourself to receive it.

To accomplish this, we use astronomy, astrology, and tools of magickal practice including tarot, crystals, candles, incantations, visualizations, and a journal. Yes—a journal. It's very important to keep track of your magickal work and it's best to have all your notes in one place. Plus, all words are magick words, so journals fit right in here. If any of this sounds unfamiliar or overwhelming, don't worry, you'll get plenty of opportunities to increase your knowledge throughout these pages. Besides, this process is about YOU. The most important thing is that you feel connected to this work, so if there's something you just can't get with, don't! The details aren't going to make or break it. What will make or break it is your dedication to the Four Principles (see page 26) and your use of each of the Four Elements (see page 28).

PART ONE

The Basics

Astronomy

For our purposes, we're sticking to the basics. Strictly speaking, you don't *need* to know the astronomy behind what we're working with, but I find it very helpful. The foundation of a magickal year is formed by the positions of three celestial bodies—the Earth, Moon, and Sun. These are the bodies that affect our bodies most directly. Their movement determines the new moon, full moon, summer and winter solstices, and vernal and autumnal equinoxes. This is plenty to work with—enough for a complete life revolution. For fun, we'll also talk about lunar and solar eclipses and we'll even break our own rules and stray just a bit from the basics to touch on Mercury retrograde. But that's for later. Right now, let's look at how these events come to be.

New Moon

The new moon (also known as the dark moon) occurs when the Earth, Sun, and Moon are all aligned with the Moon between the Earth and the Sun. In this position, the face of the Moon we see on Earth is completely turned away from the Sun, leaving it dark.

Full Moon

At the full moon, the position of the Earth and Moon are reversed, with the Earth standing between the Sun and the Moon, allowing the Sun to illuminate the entirety of the half of the Moon we can see from here.

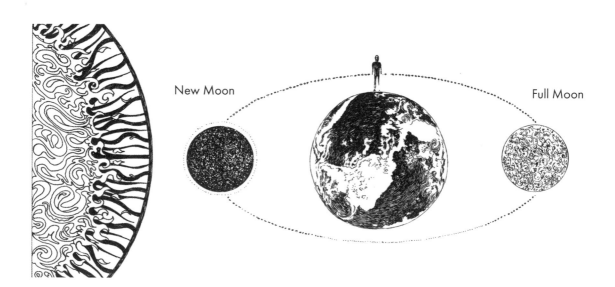

New Moon

Full Moon

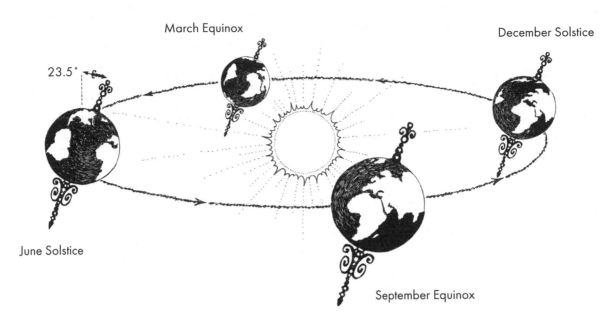

March Equinox

December Solstice

23.5°

June Solstice

September Equinox

Solstices and Equinoxes

Because the Earth's axis is tilted 23.5 degrees, the part of the Earth facing the Sun changes throughout the year as the Earth travels around the Sun. This is what causes the seasons.

The summer solstice, June 21 in the Northern Hemisphere (see opposite regarding the Southern Hemisphere), occurs when the north pole is tilted most toward the Sun. The winter solstice, December 21 in the Northern Hemisphere, occurs when the North Pole is tilted most away from the Sun.

The equinoxes occur when—you guessed it—the tilt of Earth causes the light of the Sun to fall equally on both hemispheres. The vernal (spring) equinox marks the halfway point between the winter and summer solstices, when the days are growing longer, March 22 in the Northern Hemisphere. The autumnal (fall) equinox marks the halfway point between the summer and winter solstices, when the days are getting shorter, September 22 in the Northern Hemisphere.

The Southern Hemisphere

The dates of the solstices and equinoxes are reversed in the Southern Hemisphere, i.e.:

Vernal equinox: September 22
Summer solstice: December 21
Autumnal equinox: March 22
Winter solstice: June 21

Due to a combination of our imperfect calendar system and the fact that the Earth wobbles on its axis, the dates of the solstices and equinoxes change from year to year, but remain roughly around the dates given here.

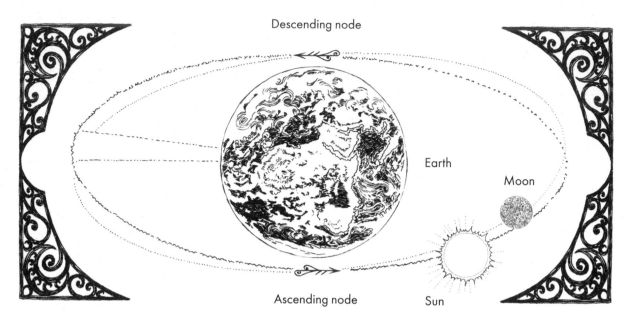

Descending node

Earth

Moon

Ascending node

Sun

Solar and Lunar Eclipses

Solar eclipses occur when our view of the Sun is blocked by a new moon; lunar eclipses occur when our view of a full moon is blocked by the Earth moving between the Sun and the Moon. Eclipses do not occur at every new and full moon, because the orbit of the Moon around the Earth is at a 5-degree tilt from the orbit of the Earth around the Sun (the apparent path of the Sun as seen from Earth). This means that eclipses can only happen when the Moon is at one of its two nodes, the points where the orbit of the Moon crosses the orbit of the Earth and the alignment of all is exact.

There are partial and full eclipses, and they are grouped together in cycles. How an eclipse looks depends on where you are on Earth at the time of the eclipse, so it is a rare treat to have a view of a total eclipse.

Because the path of totality is so narrow, for most places on Earth, seeing a total solar eclipse is a once-in-a-century event.

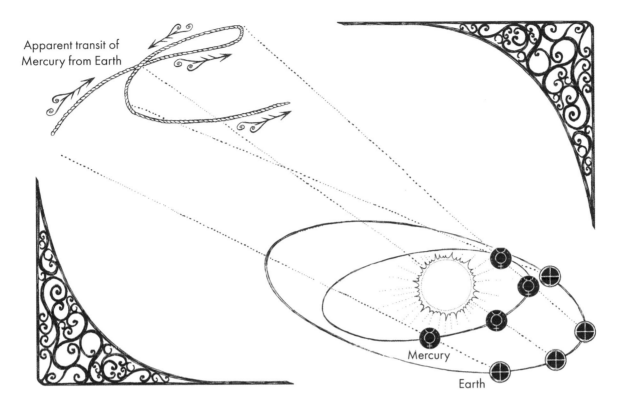

Apparent transit of
Mercury from Earth

Mercury

Earth

Mercury Retrograde

There is one other transit that looms so large in the public imagination that we have to talk about it—Mercury retrograde. Three or four times a year, Mercury reaches a place in its orbit where it appears to move backward in the sky from our vantage point on Earth. When this happens, we say that Mercury "stations retrograde." Find out more on what that means on page 17.

Other Transits

There are many other transits happening all the time as the planets of our solar system and a few large asteroids make their way through the sky. When two planets or bodies align, we say they are conjunct. Planets can form squares, trines, oppositions, and many more formations that describe their mathematical distance and position relative to each other.

Astrology

So, what does all this movement mean? That's where astrology comes in. Humans have been tracking the movement of the planets through the stars for the purpose of predicting outcomes and gaining insight for thousands of years. The way we'll be using astrology is not for the prediction of events, but for anticipating energetic waves so we can take advantage of their influence instead of fighting it.

The movement of the planets, Sun, Moon, and key asteroids through the twelve signs of the zodiac creates an overall "vibe." How that vibe interacts with our personal natal chart dictates the specific way in which we experience it. So, while we all have our own personal astrological makeup, determined by the time and place of our birth, we also experience collective astrological influence. Personal astrology is a vast world of enrichment and fascination and there are many resources available should you choose to pursue those teachings. Here, we are working with collective astrology and how we can apply it to our current experience and situation.

The zodiac wheel depicts the twelve signs along with their element.

Signs of the Zodiac

Our modern system of Western astrology, based on twelve constellations assigned to astrological signs, has been in use for approximately 2,000 years, though many of the constellations are much older. When we say today that a planet is in a sign, what we mean is the planet is in the 30-degree section of a 360-degree map of the sky assigned to that sign where the corresponding constellation was located at the time of the assignment of the sections.

In collective astrology, these attributes apply not to individual personalities, but to the energy and area of life they draw out and best support in all of us.

Generally speaking, Fire signs encourage bold action, Water signs emotional introspection, Air signs intellectual curiosity, and Earth signs grounded stability. These combine with the modalities to bring us different ways of operating within the element. Cardinal signs call for leadership, Fixed for perseverance, and Mutable for understanding.

	Fire	Water	Air	Earth
Cardinal	Aries	Cancer	Libra	Capricorn
Fixed	Leo	Scorpio	Aquarius	Taurus
Mutable	Sagittarius	Pisces	Gemini	Virgo

Seasons of the Zodiac

This book is organized according to the Sun's progression through the zodiac, referring to the time the Sun spends in each sign as that sign's season. During a sign's season, the Sun beams that astrological influence down on us, allowing us to take it in and apply it to our lives. In addition to the Sun's apparent position relative to the stars, there are two astrological events in each season of particular note—the new moon and full moon.

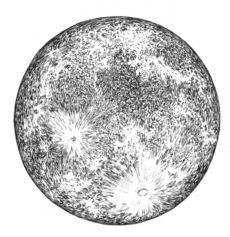

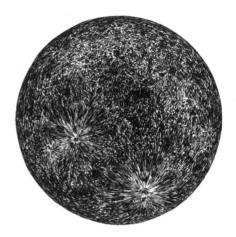

Full moons

Full moons are for seeing and for letting go. The full moon of each season is in the opposite sign of the zodiac to the one the Sun is in. When the Sun and Moon are in opposite signs, the full moon illuminates the particular dynamic or tension between those signs. Emotions can run high for the few days around full moons. Feelings that can no longer be ignored are pulled up to the surface of our consciousness so we can process them. As the Moon wanes from full down to new, it pulls away any energetic debris we are ready to let go of.

New moons

New moons offer new beginnings. The new moon of each season is in the same sign as the Sun. When the Sun and the Moon come together in a sign, we have a chance for a reset in the area of life ruled by that sign. New moons can help us bring our internal and external experiences into alignment, launch new ventures, and put fresh enthusiasm behind efforts that may need a little boost. The Moon appears dark in the sky at the time of the new moon and as the tiny crescent appears and waxes to full, the seeds we planted in the dark grow with it.

Eclipses

Solar and lunar eclipses are like extreme versions of the new and full moons they fall on. Solar eclipses offer a hard reset, like restarting electronics, while lunar eclipses bring final endings, often to longstanding issues. Because eclipses are extreme versions of the lunar cycle they fall on, it is appropriate to use the rituals provided in this book on those days. Adjust by setting your focus on something big and something internal. Eclipses offer opportunities for major transformations, even revolutions, and they don't come around very often.

Solstices and equinoxes

The solstices are like the full and new moon for the entire year. At the summer solstice, the longest day of the year, the light is most plentiful, similar to the full moon. The sun shines down on everything we need to know and see so we can clear out what we don't need before the days begin growing shorter as we head into autumn, then winter. At the winter solstice, the dark is most plentiful, similar to the new moon. The winter solstice is the longest night of the year, allowing us the time and space to look deep within and discover what we want to grow as the days lengthen heading toward spring and summer.

The equinoxes are the two points of the year when we have literal and energetic balance between day and night. They are the tipping points between the solstices and we celebrate them as milestones marking our progress through the year. At the autumnal equinox, we welcome the introspection of the lengthening dark nights and at the vernal equinox, we celebrate the blooming of the light.

Mercury retrograde

The most widely feared and loathed transit. Mercury rules communication, so when it goes into apparent retrograde motion, yes, wires can get crossed. However, there is an upside. Every Mercury retrograde period brings us new information that updates an old story and facilitates growth and healing. Just be sure to backup your hard drives and give yourself an extra half hour to get anywhere.

Solstices and Equinoxes Ritual

The four turning points of the year are important times of reflection and planning. Mark these days by doing the simple three-card tarot reading opposite. Journal afterward about what your reading means to you, considering what specific events, thoughts, or feelings the cards are speaking to you about and how they can guide you. End by lighting a candle as you set your intentions for the coming three months.

1 How you have grown over the past three months

2 A lesson to take forward

3 What to pay attention to over the coming three months

Magick

The practice of magick is as old as civilization and just as diverse. When you say "bless you" after someone sneezes, you are practicing a form of magick, reciting an incantation meant to keep that person safe from harm. Wear a special piece of jewelry to feel powerful for a big meeting? That's a talisman. And the special soup you make when someone is sick is a kind of potion.

There is nothing inherently scary or dangerous about practicing magick. Just like most things in life, it's all in the attitude. Approach magick with the intention of deepening understanding and encouraging empowerment of yourself and others, focus on your own work, and leave others to theirs. Magick is an expression of your personal relationship with yourself, your guides, the Earth, elements, universe, and all that is divine. Treat it with reverence and love.

Because magick is something so personal, it is important that you work with it in a way that feels right to you. If you have a deep aversion to open flame of any sort, then candles are not

for you! Omit them. Follow the rest of the ritual. Have trouble with visualization? Try reading those passages out loud or writing down your version. Will these changes affect the ritual? Yes, of course, but it is better for you to feel connected to the work. Make an effort to follow as much as you can and allow yourself to make personal accommodations. As you make your way through this book, you may find yourself growing more comfortable with some aspects and adding them back in. And since you can repeat this work year after year, you will have plenty of chances to explore various ways to engage with it.

Some Magickal Ground Rules

1

Your magick is for you

Respect the free will of others and keep your spells to yourself.

2

Your magick contributes to the greater good

Maintaining a mindset of "for the good of all beings" tells the Universe that you are not only in this for yourself, but as an engaged citizen of the world.

3

Your magick is a request and a suggestion

The Divine, however you frame it, has the final say on what will be most beneficial for you at this time.

4

Your magick is working

Even if you can't see it, even if it really doesn't seem like it. See previous rule.

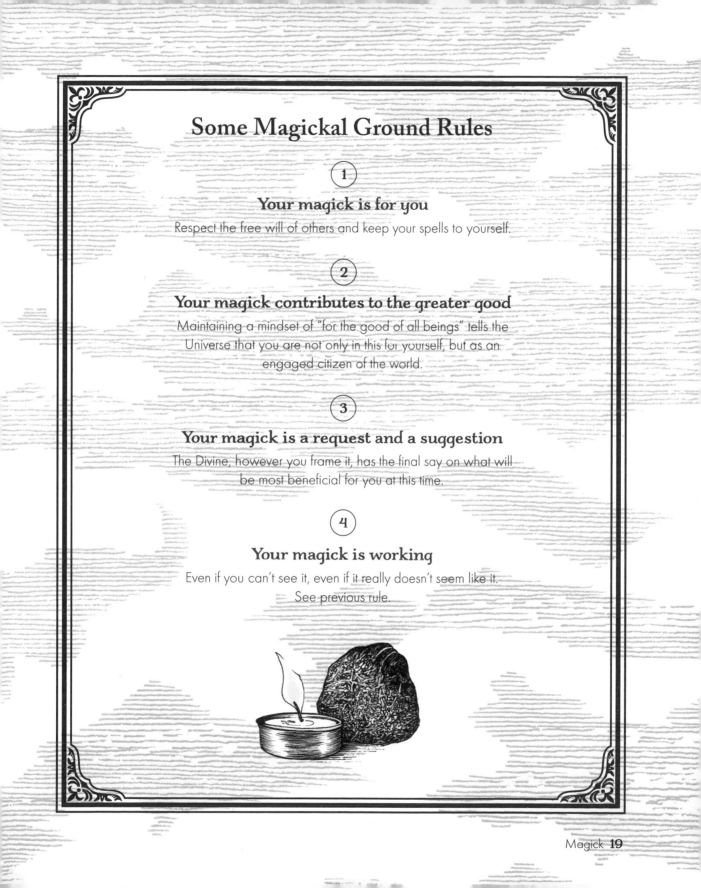

Tools and Tips

Before you get started on your transformative project of magick, there are some essentials you will need to get familiar with. They will be your trusted companions as you work your way through the seasons.

Tarot Cards

These are the primary means of conversing with your subconscious, your guides, and the Divine. Choose a deck that speaks to you. There is no "best" deck for beginners. The best deck is the one that you naturally connect with. Keep in mind that we will be working with the full 78-card tarot deck with traditional card names. The meanings and images referenced in this book are from *Elemental Power Tarot* (CICO Books, 2020).

Care of your deck

Treat your tarot deck with love and respect, as you would a trusted friend. Store it in a place of honor. You can keep a piece of selenite with your cards to keep their energy clear. Only lay your cards out on a clean, dry place, preferably either on a surface or a cloth reserved only for readings. Keep them out of direct sunlight to avoid photo-bleaching the exposed cards.

Use in rituals

Each ritual in this book calls for the use of tarot card imagery. If you have more than one deck, you can reserve one for use in ritual. Otherwise, make copies or drawings of the cards for your rituals and keep the actual cards in your deck for your readings.

Readings

When you sit down to do a reading, make sure you have plenty of time and a calm mind and have your journal and pen ready (see page 22).

1 Clear the energy (see page 22) and get comfortable.

2 Think about the spread you are about to do and open yourself to all information that will be helpful to you.

3 Shuffle the cards until they feel "done," or at least three times.

4 Cut the deck into two piles, put the bottom one on the top, then cut the deck again into three piles. Choose the pile you are most drawn to. (Alternatively, you can fan the entire deck out and choose cards individually.)

5 Lay out the cards and take a few minutes to gather your overall impressions as well as those of the individual cards and positions.

6 Notate the spread with the date, spread, position numbers, and card titles, and your thoughts and impressions in your journal.

Some of the spreads in this book call for you to choose a card from the deck for one of the positions. If you do not feel sure about which card to choose, read through the card meanings in your guidebook to find one that most closely matches what is called for.

Getting cozy with your deck

You do not need to have any experience with tarot cards to begin using them with this work. However, if you'd like to get more familiar with the cards, here is a simple daily practice to

kickstart your learning. You may want to keep a separate notebook for this exercise.

1 Clear the energy (see page 22) and get comfortable.

2 Shuffle the cards with a clear mind—do NOT ask a question.

3 Fan the cards out in front of you, facing down. You should be able to see a little bit of the back of most of the cards.

4 Choose a card and turn it over. This is your lesson for the day! Note which card you pulled and your general impressions of it BEFORE looking up its meaning.

5 Look up the card in your guidebook or tarot reference and note what pops out for you.

6 Write a paragraph or two about a time, situation, or event in your life that this card relates to.

Daily repetition of this exercise will help considerably with forming a personal relationship to the language of tarot. If you keep getting repeat cards, feel free to pull a different card for that day, but note in your writing which card you pulled first.

Journal

In addition to the journaling prompts given for each season, it is recommended that you make notes on your rituals and your intentions and circumstances at the time you perform them. Treat yourself to a journal or notebook you enjoy writing in and use it only for these exercises. This will be the start of your own personal grimoire—a book of magickal spells.

If you already keep a journal, continue that practice in a separate book and be sure to date all entries for ease of cross-referencing.

There are a couple of instances in this book that call for multiple colors of pens or highlighters, but the majority of your entries can be written in any pen or pencil you like.

Energy Clearing Tools

Clearing and setting the energy of your space is an essential skill and practice for magickal work. There are three main ways to accomplish this: with smoke, a spray, or a bell. Begin by physically tidying your space and turning off all electronics, including your phone, so you can keep your focus on creating sacred space. Then, open the windows and begin your energetic cleansing. No matter which method you use, hitting all four corners of each room ensures a thorough cleansing. I suggest doing a full house cleanse at least once a month, preferably on the full moon. You can do touch ups in your altar, meditation, or journaling areas as needed.

Smoke

Smoke cleansing is the practice of burning dried sacred plants to cleanse and set the energy and create a divine atmosphere. The most commonly used smoke cleansers are sage and Palo Santo.

However, with the skyrocketing popularity of the metaphysical world, there are issues with ethical harvesting and use of these plants that are essential to the religious practice of many Indigenous Peoples, particularly in the Americas. If you choose to use smoke for clearing energy, buy ethically sourced materials.

Spray

There are a number of sprays on the market made specifically for energy clearing. You can find sprays created from a single ingredient, such as sage or Palo Santo spray, or multiple ingredients formulated for a specific intention. Sprays are wonderful for people with smoke sensitivities and are more environmentally friendly than smoke as they use much less of the plant.

Bell

Ringing a bell is a common form of clearing out undesirable energy in many Eastern traditions as well as in witchcraft. Any bell that has a tone pleasing to your ear is great. Find one you like and keep it with your altar supplies, using it only for this purpose.

Fire Safety

For all rituals, you will be asked to let your candles burn until they go out on their own. If this makes you uncomfortable, don't do it. Our goal is for you to gain insight and feel empowered, not to live in fear.

Set your altar in a fire-safe place. If you have a fireplace, that's perfect. If not, choose a non-flammable surface. Decorative metal trays are a great option. Be sure your altar has plenty of clearance on all sides and nothing hanging above.

If you do not feel comfortable leaving a candle burning overnight, you have two options. You can use tea candles instead (they burn out in just a few hours) or you can cover the candle to snuff the flame at night and light it again with intention when you wake up. NEVER blow out a candle you are using in a ritual.

Candles

You will use three types of candles throughout the year: seven-day ritual, tea, and taper.

Seven-day ritual candles

These are the tall kind in glass that come in a variety of colors. Some metaphysical shops sell them pre-dressed or will dress them for you. Ideally, get them plain and dress them yourself according to the ritual (see page 25).

Tea candles

The small kind in a little metal base you can usually buy in packs of 100 are great. Make sure they are unscented and that they have a little container or base to avoid getting wax everywhere.

Taper candles

Most familiar as the candles you would put in holders on your dinner table, these are tall and thin with a wider base tapering up to a very narrow top. They come in a variety of colors, but the plain white ones will work best for our purposes. Get the standard width (about 1 inch/ 2.5 cm) and a low height (6 inches/15 cm is fine). The taller the candle, the longer it's going to take to burn.

Crystals

Crystals are used in most of the rituals in this book. When they are not on your altar, you can carry one in your pocket to give you a little boost of the energy you need. To charge and cleanse your crystals, give them a good rinse under running water and leave them out under the full moon—either outside or by a window where they can see her glow.

Crystals used in this book

Amethyst—purification, gentle protection

Angelite—communication with guides

Aquamarine—calm outlook, clear communication

Black obsidian—releasing sorrow

Black tourmaline—clearing, protection

Blue kyanite—psychic abilities

Blue lace agate—clear communication

Carnelian—courage, vitality

Chrysocolla—nurturing, unconditional love

Citrine—motivation, enthusiasm

Clear apophyllite—enlightenment

Fluorite (any color)—mental focus and clarity

Green aventurine—abundance

Green calcite—calm, serenity

Hematite—grounding

Iolite—journeying

Labradorite—activation of magickal abilities

Lapis lazuli—inner vision

Lemurian seed quartz crystal—transmission of ancient teachings

Lepidolite—soothing

Malachite—good fortune

Moss agate—connection to Earth, regeneration

Nuummite—amplification of magickal abilities

Orange calcite—creativity, happiness

Peacock ore—balance, joy

Peridot—luck, positivity

Pyrite—confidence, creativity

Quartz crystal—amplification of intention

Red garnet—enjoyment of Earthly life

Rhodochrosite—self-love and acceptance

Rose quartz—love

Ruby—passion, enthusiasm

Selenite—spiritual connection, energetic cleansing

Sodalite—dedication, perseverance

Other Supplies

The following herbs, oils, and other materials are used in the rituals in this book—some for candle dressings, some for offerings, some for both.

Herbs and other magickal ingredients

Cayenne pepper—leadership, drive
Cinnamon sticks—magickal powers
Dill—focus, vision
Honey—hope, longevity
Lavender—calm
Licorice tea—soothing, protection
Mint (fresh)—happiness
Nutmeg (whole)—personal development

Parsley (fresh)—communication
Pecans—mental clarity
Rosemary—protection of the heart
Roses—love
Salt—clearing, protection
Strawberries—Freya, the Norse goddess of love, war, and magick
Sunflowers—optimism, knowledge

Oils

Frankincense—divine wisdom
Jasmine—reflection, receptivity
Olive—balance, peace
Rose—love
Sesame—clearing

Dressing Candles

You only need a tiny bit of material to dress a candle. Many of the oils and herbs we use for candle dressing are flammable and using too much could be dangerous.

For oils, just a drop is plenty. It is easier to control the amount if you put the oil on your finger, then trace it around the top of the candle. All oils should be traced around the wick three times clockwise, except sesame oil or any other oil used for clearing.

Clearing oils should be traced counterclockwise. For herbs, crumble or chop them as small as you can and sprinkle just a bit (less than would cover your pinky nail) on top of the candle.

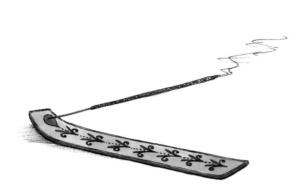

Incense

Incense comes in a variety of forms, most commonly stick or cone. Any form you like is fine. Be sure to get a corresponding incense burner.

Other materials and equipment

Small nail (for carving candles)
Small dish for water
Feather
Twine
Rocks
Small sticks
Small jars with lids
Coins
Pen and small pieces of paper
Skull figurine

The Four Principles

In order to get the most out of this work, you'll need to develop dedication to four principles. These principles will allow you to see your progress clearly, inspire hope, lift your heart, and ground you in your power. They are essential to this and any magickal work.

You are enough

Everything that makes up who you are—your hopes and dreams, your past, your fears, your present circumstances—is exactly right for this work. You are uniquely and ideally equipped and prepared to take yourself by the hand and stride over the threshold into your new world. You are smart enough, creative enough, witchy enough, experienced enough, intuitive enough, powerful enough—you get the picture. Look in the mirror. Seriously, set down the book and look in the mirror. THAT is the person, the *only* person, with the power to create the life you desire. It's only you. You are enough.

You may find it helpful to write the title of each of these principles on a note for your fridge or mirror as a visual affirmation.

You have enough

When we think about making changes in our lives, we tend to think of what we will have when the change is complete—such as houses, cars, jobs, wardrobe, or vacations. These are all great, but they are emblems of goals; they are not the goal itself. For example, maybe you believe you need a bigger house in order to feel happier. Maybe what a bigger house would provide is dedicated space for meditation or a feeling of security—and that is your true goal beneath the emblem. Emblems distract us from our true goals and can trick us into believing our goals are much further away than they actually are. This is because almost all emblems require specific material resources.

Focusing on material resources (and a lack thereof) is the easiest way to get derailed from self-transformation and evolution. You have everything you need to do what you need to do right now, today, to transform your life. Tomorrow you will have what you need tomorrow. Every day, you have enough. If you do not possess the resources to accomplish a specific step or task, then that step or task is not for today. You have enough.

Here is perfect

Wherever you are in the world, in life, is perfect. The space that you occupy is uniquely suited to bring your focus and awareness exactly where it needs to be. Sometimes you need complete zen and stillness, and that's great. Sometimes you need cramped quarters and chaos to snap something into focus—and that's great too! If you have found adequate space to read this book, you are definitely in a good place to embark on this work. Here is perfect.

Now is perfect

There is no such thing as starting a magickal year too late or too early. Whenever it is that you are reading these words is just right. Every time you open this book to gain some skills or guidance, whenever you sit down to journal, take a walk to clear your mind, set an altar, light a candle, consult your tarot cards—it's all at the perfect time. Now is perfect.

The Four Elements

To ensure a well-rounded magickal practice, you'll be working with techniques and tools tied to each of the four classical elements. These are the same elements the signs of the zodiac and the suits of tarot are divided into. Along with the overarching element of Spirit, they form the foundation of magickal practice. To differentiate the classical elements from common usage of the words, we capitalize the first letter. Most things in life can be related to more than one element and that's okay. We use the elements not to cleanly categorize, but to heighten our awareness of how they affect our lives and to make sure we honor them all in our work.

Air

Elemental Air is the realm of the head and neck. Intellect, communication, rational thought, and strategy are all aspects of Air. We call on Air in ritual by using incantations (spoken words), petitions (written words), the burning of incense, symbolic items, like feathers and ceremonial daggers, and crystals with Air-centric properties, such as those that enhance intellect or communication. Air facilitates our understanding of our past and present and allows us to communicate our future goals clearly to ourselves and the Divine. It is the element that most efficiently links the inner world with the outer.

The colors of Air are light blue and dark blue.

Fire

Elemental Fire is the realm of the gut. It rules instinct, action, intuition, and magick. We call on Fire in ritual by using candles, visualizations (conjuring a world or situation that doesn't exist outside of your mind), wands, and crystals with properties that boost Fire attributes, such as drive, courage, magickal abilities, and knowing without seeing. Fire can be difficult to identify on its own because it so readily combines with other elements. Intuitive hits combine with Air to allow greater understanding, instinctual pulls combine with Water and we experience passion. Such is the enigmatic beauty of Fire.

The colors of Fire are orange and yellow.

Try to keep your elemental connections balanced. At first, some will feel more natural than others and that's okay.

Water

Elemental Water is the realm of the heart, of emotion. We call on Water in ritual by using water, tinctures, chalices or cups, and crystals that encourage and support emotional expression and healing. Water is powerful and difficult to contain. It provides us with the means of connecting emotionally with the world around us and with ourselves. Water facilitates forgiveness, can wash away long-stuck patterns of the heart, and is often a much better indicator of the strength of a relationship than any analysis could be.

The colors of Water are pink and green.

Earth

Elemental Earth is the realm of the base of the spine and bottoms of the feet. It rules the whole of our material world and our bodies, homes, physical surroundings, and communities. We call on Earth in ritual by setting altars, imbuing physical objects with meaning, and using any crystal, but particularly those with properties that connect us with our physical world, home, and body. Earth relates to finance only because we have accepted currency as our common means of trading in material goods.

The colors of Earth are dark red and dark green.

How to Begin

Here are some things to consider before the start of your magickal year.

Timing

There is no correct time to begin this work. Whenever you feel drawn to the process is perfect. This book is arranged according to the astrological year, beginning with Aries season, but because time is both cyclical and sequential, you can jump in any time. No matter where you begin, if you keep going, you'll land on each station eventually.

The rituals, readings, and exercises in this book are designed to be used year after year. They are created to align with themes that recur with the astrological seasons and to connect these themes with your goals, intentions, and explorations. With time and dedication, the connection between the Sun and Moon, the zodiac, and your magick will become effortless. Be patient. This can take many years. But as they say, it's the journey that matters, not the destination.

Preparation

Read through the tips and tools and then through the season you are starting in and the one after that. Find out what you have and what you'll need. Locate sources for materials that are less commonly available, like ritual candles and crystals. If you have a metaphysical shop in your area, that is wonderful. If not, you can get everything you need online.

Designate an area of your home as the magickal area. This is where you will set your altar for rituals, do your tarot readings, and write your journal entries. Try to keep as many things as possible for this purpose alone. If you have a whole room in your home you can dedicate solely to magick, that is wonderful and I highly recommend it. If not, do what makes sense for your life—a table that is only for tarot readings, a chair used only for magickal writing. Anything that needs to serve multiple purposes should be cleansed before each magickal use.

Choose a location and base for your altar. You will be lighting candles and letting them burn for long periods of time. It is essential that your altar be located in a place that is fire safe (see page 23).

Execution

Now you're ready to begin! I'm sure you have questions. Here are a few answers.

Q: I really need to work on my career, but it's Cancer season and that's all about emotion. What do I do?

If the urgent need to do magickal work on your career comes up during Cancer season, there is likely some aspect of your emotional relationship with your career or work that needs tending in order to move forward. When you engage in your magickal practice, center your relationship with your career in your workings.

This is true for any seemingly incongruous pairing of urgent issue and season. The seasons do not dictate what issues will come up in our lives; they provide us with a lens through which to view them.

Q: What if I can't get a certain item for a ritual?

That's okay. If you can't get one thing, you can move forward with the rest of the ritual or substitute something similar. If you are unsure what a suitable substitution would be, just leave that item out. It's better to be missing an herb or crystal than to add one in that doesn't match the intention of the spell.

Q: I live in a situation where it is unsafe or not possible for me to have a visible altar. Can I still do this work?

Yes! Whatever works for you is perfect. I've included a range of exercises for each season to make this book accessible. Maybe when you start out, you could stick to the journaling, then later you might add in the tarot spreads. Or if you are interested in crystals, you may be more comfortable carrying one in your pocket and seeing how it goes before arranging several of them around a candle. That is all okay. This book is for you. Engage with whichever parts of it resonate most with you. The rest will be waiting for you when you're ready.

Q: I have a hard time thinking of what to write. Can I skip the writing?

The writing is the one thing you should avoid skipping with everything you've got (the tarot readings are a very close second). Find a way in. Don't like writing by hand? Write your journal on a computer or even speak it into a recorder, then run the audio through a transcription program. This is the one thing that requires no special equipment or knowledge. It's something you already know how to do. Dig in.

If you find yourself experiencing extreme writer's block, you are putting too much pressure on yourself to do the exercise "correctly." Remember there is no right or wrong way. There is your way.

Q: Will this make me a witch?

Only if you're lucky! Just kidding—yes, it definitely will. Welcome!

PART TWO

The Seasons
of the Zodiac

ARIES

CARDINAL

FIRE

Aries Season

MARCH 21–APRIL 19 • CARDINAL FIRE • I AM...

Aries is symbolized by the ram, that fierce defender of vast mountain territories —or, really, anything it considers its own. Domestic rams are just as fierce as their wild counterparts. It's not a survival thing, it's just inherent in their beings. As the first sign in the zodiac, Aries is a natural leader, whether by rallying others to their cause or quietly setting an example of unapologetic individuality.

In Aries, autonomy and natural instincts for leadership are lit up by the warm blaze of Cardinal Fire. You are called to reflect on who you are and what you represent. The old roles no longer fit and the need for autonomy is great. The ability to self-actualize is dependent on the ability to make choices freely. While we are all living within our own unique set of circumstances that support and limit different areas of our lives, it is our freedom to choose what to do *within those circumstances* that makes us autonomous beings. Paradoxically, independence is often compromised by too much focus on pushing boundaries. This can keep you focused on defiance, a state that ties you to a real or imagined adversary and distracts you from your own evolution. Drawing that rebellion inward and allowing it to fuel the fire of your own personal expression is the key to developing a leadership style in line with your values.

Leadership is a natural outgrowth of individuality. There are many styles of leadership. You don't have to be standing on a stage with a microphone and an agenda to be a leader (though if that's your thing, get up there!). In fact, many of the most effective leaders possess a quiet power, inspiring others with the gravity of their presence. A refusal to conform to unhealthy standards, a radical expression of self, remaining calm under pressure, treating others with kindness, and setting and maintaining loving boundaries are all forms of leadership that often go under the radar, drowned out by loud voices and bold moves. Yet, they are often the most effective at creating meaningful change.

Relationships, too, are unsung heroes of personal growth. Forming deep connections with others may seem the antithesis of autonomy, but individual sovereignty is needed for any form of alliance to thrive. The ability of all parties to

Aries season is a time to affirm your independence and your identity, within yourself and out in the world.

accurately identify their own strengths and weaknesses, as well as those of their partner(s), is directly related to the health of the relationship. This insight is impossible without a strong sense of self. Seeing yourself clearly as an individual is a prerequisite for understanding a potential or current relationship. Aries season is a great time to examine and clear out any urges to conform to what you think another person wants you to be.

The Sun moves through Aries just after the vernal equinox in the Northern Hemisphere and just after the autumnal equinox in the Southern Hemisphere (see page 11), one of the two points in the year when day and night are equal. While the Sun travels through Aries, set your sights on revolutionizing your idea of who you are and can be in the world.

Aries in Tarot

Aries is associated with The Emperor, the dynamic commander of the tarot. The Emperor invites us to take charge without taking advantage and to model the behavior we'd like to see in others. Think more "leading with love" and less "my way or the highway." The authority of The Emperor is undeniable and can be intoxicating. Use responsibly.

Aries' ruling planet, Mars, is associated with The Tower. Here we see the need to break with stale standards, which is required for the highest incarnation of The Emperor to come to life.

The Emperor

The Tower

Aries Season Activities

- Asking for a raise
- Updating your personal style
- Setting boundaries with partners
- Laughing the loudest
- Having an uncomfortable conversation
- Standing up for someone

- Wearing red (bonus points for red lipstick)
- Eating spicy food
- Hatching a daring plan
- Painting a self portrait

Aries Season Journaling

Write for 20 minutes a day, filling in the blank of the very Aries declaration,

"I am _____ ."

If 20 minutes is overwhelming, try ten or five. Maybe weekly journaling is better for you.

Whatever works for you is perfect. See if you can take the statement in different directions, as in the examples opposite.

Pushing yourself to embody these various ideas as you write will reveal and refine the You that is yearning to be seen.

Exploring core identities

"I am a witch"
"I am from Minnesota"

Current activities

"I am writing"
"I am looking out the window at a bird"

Desired activities or identities

"I am swimming with whale sharks"
"I am a best-selling author"

Aries Season Tarot Spread

This tarot spread explores the core focus of Aries season, identity. Use it as part of your journaling practice or simply to get some insight into your personal focus for the season, week, or day. If you are new to tarot, you may find it helpful to remove the pip cards (Ace–Ten) from the deck for this spread.

1 Who you are; what your identity is focused on at this time

2 What you are invited to integrate at this time

3 Who you aspire to be, your ideal self

4 Who you fear you are, your shadow self

Sample reading

The carefree part of you, taking life as it comes, has served you well. You have an ease and adaptability about you that may come off as naive to some, but is actually hard-won wisdom. Informed trust in yourself has served you well.

Now you are invited to send down roots to ground all that you've learned and begin to build something out of it. You'll be surprised by how much you can accomplish when you put the work in. The challenge is maintaining follow-through. Finish what you start and you won't be disappointed.

The vision you aspire to have for your life can be brought into focus through this work. Sometimes we need to start the work to clearly see what it is forming or leading us toward. The steps you take now will feed your greater goals and help them develop.

A fear of dependency may lead you to reject partnerships. It's okay to value independence and autonomy. Take some time to reflect on where your aversion to partnership comes from and see if you can find some healing around that.

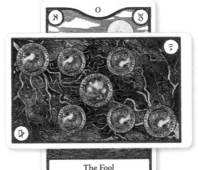

The Fool

The Lovers

Cards pulled

1 The Fool

2 Seven of Coins

3 King of Coins

4 The Lovers

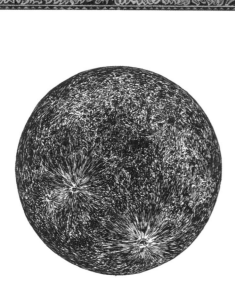

SUN   ARIES   ARIES   MOON

New Moon: Sun in Aries, Moon in Aries

The new moon in Aries is our annual invitation to step boldly into personal power, take the lead, and set daring and courageous goals in our work and personal lives.

How have you kept yourself or your work small to avoid upsetting the status quo? Are there internalized barriers holding you back from filling in all the details of your ultimate vision for your life? Is there something you want to see in the world that no one else can or is willing to provide? If you could lead others to invest their time and energy in one thing, what would it be? The greatest leadership depends on inspiration and motivation. To lead effectively, you must deeply believe in what you are asking others to devote their resources to—this includes you!

The ritual for this new moon is designed to awaken and amplify the core strength that is your offering to the world, and to light the torch of this strength to lead the way.

New Moon Ritual

Gather what you have of the following:

- Smoke, spray, or bell
- Orange seven-day ritual candle
- Printout or drawing of The Emperor card
- Selection of crystals—carnelian, ruby, or orange calcite, and selenite (if you don't have these, feel free to improvise with what you have on hand, keeping within the orange/red color spectrum)
- Lavender oil and cayenne pepper

1 Clear the energy of your space (see page 22), then close your eyes and take three deep, cleansing breaths to ground yourself.

2 Place the candle in the center of your altar area with the image of The Emperor in front (closest to you). Place the crystals around the altar area in a pattern of your choosing.

3 Place a drop of lavender oil on top of the candle and trace it around three times clockwise, then sprinkle a tiny bit of cayenne pepper on top (see page 25).

4 Light the candle and say,

"As I step into my calling as a leader, all doubt falls away and I am filled with joy and motivation."

5 Close your eyes and spend a few minutes settling into your body. Notice how your limbs arrange themselves to keep you stable, how your breath automatically works to fill your blood with the oxygen you need. See if you can feel the oxygen enter your bloodstream and flow out into your body, pouring strength and vitality into every cell. Then, notice a bright orange flame burning in the core of your body. Take some time to gaze admiringly at this flame with your mind's eye—watch its movement, feel its warmth. When you are ready, reach into your body and take the flame in your hand, then place your other hand over it. A transformation takes place, hidden in your hands. Open them back up and see what remains. Is it an object? A message? A being? What does it mean to you? How does it make you feel? Make a mental note of this. Stay in this world as long as you like, then gently open your eyes and write down what you found in your hands in your journal with your ritual notes.

6 Leave the candle burning (see page 23) and repeat the visualization in Step 5 daily for seven days. If you are using tea candles, dress and light a new one each day and repeat the incantation in Step 4.

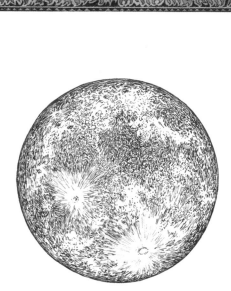

SUN | ARIES | LIBRA | MOON

Full Moon: Sun in Aries, Moon in Libra

The full moon of Aries season is in the opposite sign of Libra. The full moon in Libra is our annual opportunity to balance our needs with those of others.

The axis of Aries/Libra highlights how we navigate independence and relationships. What we were taught as children about how to behave in friendship and romance, how much autonomy we were given, and whether we were encouraged to conform or rebel all influence how we experience connection with others. These patterns stick. The full moon in Libra illuminates which of these patterns we need to be aware of so we can gently release what is no longer serving our emotional health and long-term growth.

The ritual for this full moon is designed to balance your independence with your interdependence, opening a path forward toward harmony, love, and fulfillment in all relationships—including your relationship with yourself. For this to happen, habits, concepts, and patterns that create discord will fall away as the Moon wanes.

Full Moon Ritual

Gather what you have of the following:

- Smoke, spray, or bell
- Carnelian, rose quartz, selenite, and quartz crystal
- Printouts or drawings of The Emperor and Justice cards
- Two seven-day ritual candles —one orange, one blue
- Olive oil and cayenne pepper

1 Clear the energy of your space (see page 22), then close your eyes and take three deep, cleansing breaths to ground yourself.

2 Set your altar as follows:

Center: selenite and quartz crystal
Left: The Emperor, orange candle, carnelian
Right: Justice, blue candle, rose quartz

3 Place a drop of olive oil on top of each candle and trace it around three times clockwise, then sprinkle a tiny bit of cayenne pepper on top (see page 25).

4 Light the candles and say,

"I am full of love and compassion for myself and others and make peace with all that has formed who I am."

5 Close your eyes and spend a few minutes finding the most complete stillness you can. Breathe in for four counts, out for four counts for four full cycles. Then breathe in for three counts, out for three counts for three full cycles, then in for two, out for two for two cycles. Finally finish with one deep, long inhale, filling your entire being with your breath and exhaling all of the air out of your lungs completely. Bring your awareness to your heart. Breathing normally, find a flicker of light in the center of your heart and grow it with every breath until your entire being is filled with the light of your heart. Then gently bring your consciousness back to the present, bringing this light with you, and open your eyes.

6 Leave the candles burning (see page 23) and repeat the visualization in Step 5 daily for seven days. If you are using tea candles, dress and light a new one each day and repeat the incantation in Step 4.

TAURUS

FIXED

EARTH

Taurus Season

APRIL 20 – MAY 20 • FIXED EARTH • I VALUE...

Taurus is symbolized by the bull: powerful, content until provoked, master of their domain. As the Fixed Earth sign of the zodiac, the influence of Taurus arguably holds more inertia than any other sign. Once a habit is set or a source of comfort secured in a Taurean sphere, it is very difficult to change. We use bulls as a symbol of stubbornness, calling those set in their ways bullheaded, but we can just as easily frame this quality as resolute or determined and see it for the asset it can be.

Perseverance and tenacity are great virtues when applied to pursuing what you truly desire and admire, but these goals and values shift over time. We need to check in periodically to identify what we are driving toward and whether our earthly path is still on track with our spiritual ideals. The earthly realm is commonly associated with work and finance. Contemporary culture prizes material gain over personal well-being. But we cannot achieve true prosperity without caring for our wellness and comfort.

Comfort is a tricky beast. We tend to equate comfort with soothing, but they are not the same. Soothing is a means of bringing temporary relief to a temporary injury. Comfort is long term. Comfort is steady. When you achieve comfort, you don't need as much soothing because the

small bumps don't bother you as much. Conversely, if you sustain larger bumps or more long-term bumps, trying to relieve them with soothing will lead to frustration and exhaustion. By stubbornly committing to caring for yourself— prioritizing rest, nourishing food, and a supportive home environment—you provide yourself with the foundation required to push your worldly dreams further.

When you focus on true stability there are things in your life that no longer fit: physical things, emotional things, spiritual things that cause imbalance. Ideally, deprived of energy and attention, these fall away naturally, clearing the way for abundance to thrive. The abundance cultivated under Taurus demands function. This is not a pursuit of flashy or ornate detail, no matter how beautifully done. In Taurus season, luxury is

Taurus season is a time to ensure that your daily habits and rituals are aligned with what you value most.

about how it feels in and on the body—more cashmere socks than diamond earrings. Devotion to cultivating an earthly life of stability includes emotional, mental, and spiritual stability. It includes prioritizing those practices that make you feel your humanity, your creativity, and your sensuality.

While the Sun travels through Taurus, commit to raising your bar of abundance by choosing quality over quantity.

Taurus in Tarot

Taurus is associated with The Hierophant, the great spiritual teacher of the tarot and keeper of sacred traditions. The Hierophant offers a twofold invitation—to open ourselves to receive divine teachings, and to recognize the teachings we have to share with others. A spirit of altruism guides the dedication of The Hierophant. Without this impulse, dedication atrophies into plain stubbornness.

Taurus is ruled by the planet Venus, named after the Roman goddess of beauty and associated with The Empress in tarot. The influence of Venus imbues the mundane rituals Taurus loves with a sense of grace, even performance, that betrays the depth of meaning these rituals hold.

The Hierophant

The Empress

Taurus Season Activities

- Cooking elaborate meals

- Redecorating

- Stopping to smell the roses

- Silk pajamas as daywear

- Strict adherence to a desire-based diet

- Long hours on a personal project

- Not settling

- Clarifying non-negotiables

- Unapologetic napping

- Yoga and meditation retreats

- Wearing emeralds (they are luxurious and promote prosperity)

Taurus Season Journaling

Write for ten minutes each day, focusing on one thing that you value. The subject of your writing can be a person, place, or object or it can be a feeling, a memory, a talent you possess, a virtue or personality trait, a cause, or a connection—anything that you see as holding great importance and meaning in the world, and something you would not want to live without. Try to focus on something you value in yourself at least one day each week. Honoring your own importance in the world is key to clarifying and living within your value system. When you see how you are a living example of what you hold dear, your ability to appreciate other people grows.

Decide on the subject before you begin writing. If multiple ideas come up, note them for possible subjects in later days and pick the one that speaks to you most in the moment. Then set a timer and write for ten minutes, gushing about the wonderful qualities of your subject and examining why it is important to you. Stop yourself after ten minutes even if you feel you have more to say. This will be difficult and feel counterintuitive. That's good! It means you're really tapping into something true. But you still have to stop. We want you to be excited to continue the exercise the next day, not burnt out from pouring all your enthusiasm into one session, as good as that may feel in the moment.

Taurus Season Tarot

Gain insight into what is driving you and what may be holding you back with this tarot spread. Use it weekly to touch base with how your priorities and values develop throughout the season. Try focusing on different areas of your life—career, home, family, romance. See if there are any surprising similarities or differences in your readings.

1 What your current values are based on

2 A potential distraction from focusing on what you value in your life and the world

3 What you are grounded in

4 What you can move on from

5 What you are being led toward

6 What to stay mindful of

Sample reading

Though you are skilled in navigating by your gut and taking action when needed, surrounding chaos can distract you from your spiritual development. Pause to take a breath and re-center.

You have seen all the information you need to see to move forward. You are ready to let go of the old rules and begin to build again on your own terms.

It is okay to accept help. You don't have to do it all yourself. What you have to offer the world is bigger than you alone.

The Chariot

The Sun

The Hierophant

Cards pulled

1 The Hierophant

2 Five of Wands

3 Six of Wands

4 The Sun

5 Page of Coins

6 The Chariot

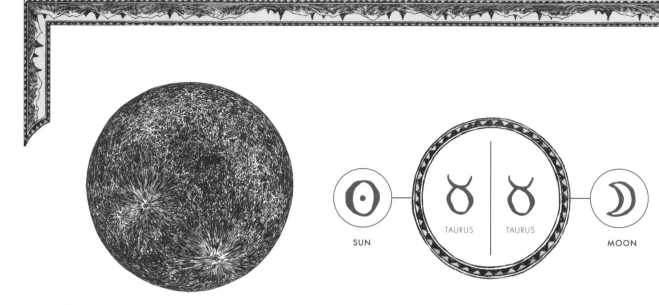

New Moon: Sun in Taurus, Moon in Taurus

The new moon in Taurus is our annual invitation to unabashedly devote ourselves to all levels of personal well-being as the ultimate foundation for an abundant life.

How do you show yourself love every day? Do you make your coffee a certain way every morning, wake up early to have some silence before the day starts, eat food that makes you feel good? Do you splurge for one pair of silk knit sweatpants over having a collection of polyester fleece? Anoint your body with oils and creams? What meaning do you attach to these actions? How do they reflect your vision of yourself as a divine being? This new moon asks you to identify which habits make you feel grounded in yourself and the Divine and then take steps to ensure they stick.

The ritual for this new moon is designed to reveal the core magick of your daily rituals and plant these seeds so they can grow deep roots in your life and psyche.

New Moon Ritual

Gather what you have of the following:

- Smoke, spray, or bell
- Small flowerpot or dish filled with dirt
- Three rose quartz and three aventurine crystals
- Three small stones, preferably from the ground near your home
- Printouts or drawings of The Hierophant and The Empress cards
- Pen
- Small dish of water

1 Clear the energy of your space (see page 22), then close your eyes and take three deep, cleansing breaths to ground yourself.

2 Place the pot of dirt in the center of your altar area and find a comfortable, seated position.

3 Arrange the rose quartz and aventurine around the base of the pot, alternating each stone.

4 Take the three small stones from the ground in your non-dominant hand, close your eyes, and feel into your body. If there is any part of you that feels uncomfortable, adjust how you are sitting until you feel completely at ease.

5 When you are settled, notice where your body touches the ground or floor. Feel how well supported you are. Allow the part(s) of your body touching the ground or floor to sprout roots and send them deep into the earth. Then notice where you can feel the air on your skin. Feel the temperature of the air, the humidity; see if you can feel how the air touches your skin. Envision divine light radiating like flames from your body and reaching up through the sky into the universe. Now feel the stones growing warm in your hand. Ask them to bring you knowledge of what three things you most need to prioritize in your daily life to be grounded in your divine self.

6 Gently open your eyes and press the stones into the pot of dirt one at a time, covering them completely.

7 On the back of the image of The Hierophant, write down three words that convey your spiritual values, then roll the paper up tightly and plant it in the pot.

8 On the back of the image of The Empress, write down three words that describe your ideal earthly life, then roll the paper up tightly and plant it in the pot.

9 Pour the water over the dirt, then set the pot outside or on a windowsill until the next full moon.

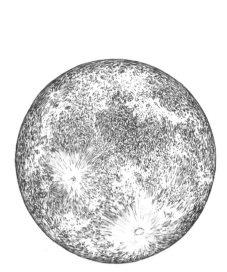

SUN   TAURUS   SCORPIO   MOON

Full Moon: Sun in Taurus, Moon in Scorpio

The full moon of Taurus season is in the opposite sign of Scorpio. The full moon in Scorpio is our annual opportunity to shine a light deep into our psyches to discover what we can no longer live with and what we truly cannot live without.

The Taurus/Scorpio axis reveals areas of tension between stability and transformation. It invites conflict between our need to ground and our need to reinvent, what sustains life and what beckons the release of death. Whatever area of life you are ready to bravely see, accept, and seriously overhaul is lit up by this moon. You may be surprised by what you see and even more so by what you feel. Know that your subconscious only brings to the surface what you possess the tools to work with. You are ready.

The ritual for this full moon is designed to help you focus your energy on what you value most,

releasing emotional attachment to things, tasks, situations, or relationships that are no longer important to you or relevant to your personal development.

Full Moon Ritual

Gather what you have of the following:

- Smoke, spray, or bell
- Printouts or drawings of The Hierophant and Death cards
- Two tea candles
- Sesame oil and frankincense oil
- Three black crystals, such as black tourmaline, black obsidian, or nuummite in any combination
- Six purple crystals—preferably amethyst, but lepidolite is also great
- Three white crystals, such as quartz crystal, clear apophyllite, Lemurian seed quartz crystal, or selenite in any combination
- One item symbolic of something you wish to release, and one item symbolic of something you wish to elevate or prioritize

1 Clear the energy of your space (see page 22), then close your eyes and take three deep, cleansing breaths to ground yourself.

2 Place the card images side by side in the center of your altar area with one tea candle in front of each.

3 Place a drop of sesame oil on the candle in front of the image of Death and trace it around the top of the candle three times counterclockwise with your finger.

4 Place a drop of frankincense oil on the candle in front of the image of The Hierophant and trace it around the top of the candle three times clockwise with your finger.

5 Arrange the black crystals and three of the purple ones in a circle around the Death card, then the white and three remaining purple crystals in a circle around The Hierophant card.

6 Place the item symbolic of something you want to release on the image of the Death card, and the item symbolic of something you want to elevate on the image of The Hierophant.

7 Light the candles and let them burn until they go out on their own (see page 23).

GEMINI

MUTABLE

AIR

♊ Gemini Season

MAY 21–JUNE 20 • MUTABLE AIR • I THINK...

Gemini is symbolized by the twins, representing duality, interaction, and the psychological separation that makes conversation, discussion, and intellectual development possible. Whether with another person or with another part of ourselves, difference is the catalyst for growth. If we were all the same, there would be little, if anything, to inspire change and evolution. The twins remind us to continually search out the other half of the equation.

The party has begun. Open your mind and your heart to interaction with people and ideas from all corners of the world. Take in their viewpoints and opinions, revel in the diversity of human experience they present. You do not have to agree with someone to accept their opinions as valid. Acceptance of others requires assuming good intentions, not assuming anything about a person's background or experience, and acknowledging your own specific frame of reference. None of us is in possession of the "standard" perspective. No one way of understanding the world is the gold-star "good" way of understanding. Let go of the need to classify ideas as good and bad and instead set a goal of gathering as much information from as many people as possible. Explore the big wide world of human thought and communication.

Increasing exposure to different points of view allows you to explore your own perspective.

Engage in conversations. See what comes up for you in response to all these new experiences and share your thoughts. The basic principle in comedy improvisation is always responding with "yes and." This means you never shoot down what another person offers, never say they are wrong. Instead, you acknowledge what they have offered and build from there. This concept works wonders for enriching conversations as well. When others feel as if you accept what they have to say (not necessarily agreeing, but accepting), they are more likely to return the favor and to expand on their thoughts in ways that might be surprising. Even if your opinion is completely counter to that of your conversation partner, using the "yes and" mode of interacting will open the conversation rather than shutting it down. It is an incredibly powerful form of interpersonal alchemy.

Another way to encourage free-flowing conversation is to practice holding space for

Gemini season is a time to get into the mix, socialize, and engage thoughtfully with other people and ideas.

others. Holding space means creating a sort of invisible protective shield that makes it safe for someone to open up and be vulnerable. There are energetic and magickal techniques for this, but you can reach the same goal with some simple words and behaviors. Listen attentively, don't interrupt, respond with supportive phrases such as "I hear you" and "I can see that," and avoid statements of judgment like "That sounds terrible," even if they seem supportive. These statements can impact the person speaking differently than intended, producing feelings of being a burden to the listener. When you do have something to say about someone's personal experience, ask first. A simple "Can I share something with you?" or "Would it be ok if I tell you how that sounds to me?" creates an atmosphere of trust and respect, inspiring deep connection.

While the Sun moves through Gemini, refine your conversational skills to deepen your connection with loved ones and strangers alike.

Gemini in Tarot

Gemini is associated with The Lovers, the card representing true balanced partnership. Interdependence, complementary skills, and mutual appreciation are all present in every true partnership, whether romantic, platonic, business, creative, or familial. When opposition comes up in life, even in the absence of conflict, it can be tempting to try to bring both sides together in resolution. This card teaches us to instead see the value in difference.

Gemini's ruling planet, Mercury, is associated with The Magician, hinting that the potential benefit of embracing complementary opposition increases exponentially when your vision extends above and beyond the sum of the parts. Believe that more is possible.

The Lovers

The Magician

Gemini Season Activities

- Chatting with strangers
- Engaging in friendly debates
- Packing out your social calendar
- Changing your mind
- Embracing your alter ego
- Dressing in contrasting colors
- Laughing through adversity
- Listening to confessional podcasts
- Going on first dates (romantic or platonic)
- Telling your story

Gemini Season Journaling

This season is all about exploring differing viewpoints and you'll be doing that by repeating this journaling exercise as often as you can. Begin with a regular journal entry—record something about your day, something that happened, something you were thinking about, a feeling that came up; whatever is front of mind for you at the moment. Then wait one day before proceeding to the next part of the exercise.

Has it been a day? Excellent. Now, read back through your entry from yesterday. Then, imagine a different way of seeing your experience. It may be easier to imagine yourself as someone else, an outside person. If you do this, try to stick to an anonymous person. Imagining a point of view for someone you know risks complicating or even damaging that relationship.

If you notice that your outside point of view tends toward the harsh, critical, or cruel, stop the exercise immediately. Take a few days off, then regroup with the specific intention of writing a differing viewpoint that is kinder and gentler than the original.

Gemini Season Tarot

Some of the most important conversations we can have are those we engage in with ourselves. This spread facilitates a conversation around a topic or situation of your choice. Choose a topic or situation, then clear your mind and lay out your spread.

1 The nature of the situation

2 Another way to look at the situation

3 Your role in the situation

4 How that role could change

5 What is under the surface of the situation

6 Another way to interpret what is under the surface

7 How you can move forward

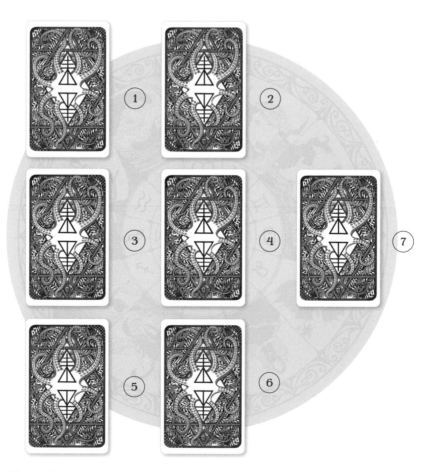

Sample reading (for a work situation)

How you think about your work is undergoing a revolution, along with the language you use to describe it. Consider how you can build and grow your work from the heart as well as the mind. You have been digging deep into your psyche to sort out what may be getting in your way, and you are now ready to use that information to your advantage.

Your connection to the powers of the Elements is strong. Visualize what you want and you just might will it into existence. Your ideas have great potential to grow and prosper if you avoid fear of lack. Believe in your own power. Develop a steady habit of creative time and trust your gut.

Judgment

The Magician

Cards pulled

1 Page of Swords

2 Queen of Coins

3 Judgment

4 The Magician

5 Ace of Coins

6 Five of Coins

7 Eight of Wands

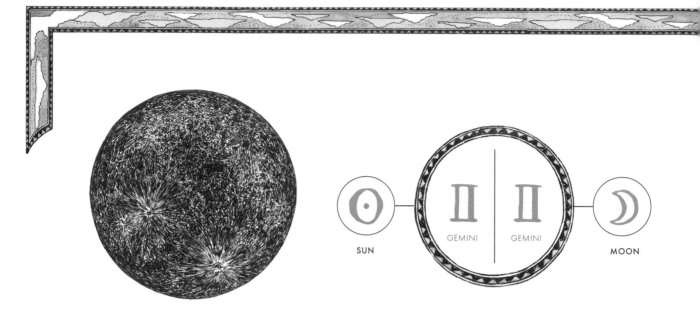

SUN — GEMINI | GEMINI — MOON

New Moon: Sun in Gemini, Moon in Gemini

The new moon in Gemini is our annual invitation to achieve depth through lightness, conversing with the Divine as it manifests in all creatures on Earth.

Idle chat is not often held in high regard, but it should be. There is no better way to find your people than by making new connections—lots of them. Small talk is only small until you get to know someone, then the conversation deepens. It is impossible to reach the depths without first wading through the shallows. Give yourself a new outlook on light conversation, framing it as the gateway to true bonding that it is. Open your mind to the experiences and attitudes of others and they will do the same for you.

The ritual for this new moon is designed to open you to new connections and encourage their organic growth, free from expectation or anticipated outcomes.

New Moon Ritual

Gather what you have of the following:

- Smoke, spray, or bell
- Printout or drawing of The Lovers card
- Candle holder or small plate
- Two pieces each of aquamarine and angelite
- Lemon
- Sharp knife and cutting board
- White taper candle
- Glass of water

1 Clear the energy of your space (see page 22), then close your eyes and take three deep, cleansing breaths to ground yourself.

2 Place the image of The Lovers in the center of your altar area with the candle holder or small plate on top of it.

3 Make a square around the candle holder/plate using the crystals to mark the corners as follows: aquamarine back left, angelite back right, angelite front left, and aquamarine front right.

4 Cut the lemon in half and coat the candle lightly in lemon juice. Put the candle in the candle holder or melt the bottom slightly to stick it to the plate.

5 Light the candle, then close your eyes and spend a few minutes feeling the joy of friendship in your heart. Begin by thinking about existing relationships that are easy and fulfilling. Then imagine the space in your heart that holds them is growing, opening, and waiting to offer and accept more wonderful relationships in your life.

6 Squeeze the rest of the lemon into a glass of water and drink it slowly while sitting with your candle.

7 Let the candle burn until it goes out on its own (see page 23).

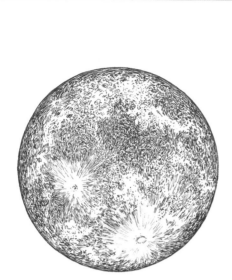

SUN   GEMINI | SAGITTARIUS   MOON

Full Moon: Sun in Gemini, Moon in Sagittarius

The full moon of Gemini season is in the opposite sign of Sagittarius. The full moon in Sagittarius is our annual opportunity to remove all obstacles blocking our acute vision into the future.

The Gemini/Sagittarius axis asks us to make sure we have considered every angle and point of view before setting our sights on one particular goal. In our eagerness to race toward accomplishment, it can be easy to overlook key information that can help us avoid missteps. Pausing to look at the whole field of possibilities helps to identify and navigate around any potential issues before they develop into insurmountable problems.

The ritual for this full moon is designed to help you widen your vision before narrowing your focus.

Full Moon Ritual

Gather what you have of the following:

- Smoke, spray, or bell
- Green seven-day ritual candle
- Printout or drawing of King of Wands card
- Hematite and malachite
- Small dish
- Pecans

1 Clear the energy of your space (see page 22), then close your eyes and take three deep, cleansing breaths to ground yourself.

2 Place the candle in the rear center of your altar area with the image of the King of Wands centered in front of it. Set the hematite to the left of the image and the malachite to the right.

3 Light the candle, then gaze into the flame and try to clear your mind completely. Let the flame be your only point of focus, and notice how your peripheral awareness can expand when you soften your gaze. Silently ask the flame to burn away anything that is obscuring your ability to see all the information you need to move forward. Close your eyes and take three more deep breaths, breathing in the flame and breathing out the ashes of the obstacles it burns.

4 Gently open your eyes and place the small dish on the image. Place the pecans inside the dish and say,

"I give this offering in thanks for the clarity of vision and passion for action of the King of Wands welcomed into my being."

5 Let the candle burn until it goes out on its own (see page 23), then discard the pecans.

CANCER

CARDINAL

▽

WATER

Cancer Season

JUNE 21–JULY 22 • CARDINAL WATER • I LOVE...

Cancer is symbolized by the crab, armored warrior of love, scurrying in the deepest depths of the sea of emotion. The hard shell and quick pincers of the crab provide the security needed to blaze new bold trails into uncharted emotional territories. As fiercely vulnerable as it is protective, the Cancerian crab is a master of loving fearlessly and nurturing freely.

Nurturing comes in many forms. Our needs vary greatly depending on who, what, where, and when we are. To truly care for ourselves and others in a way that is beneficial, we need to be always aware of the shifting emotional tides and ready to respond to them in real time. True caregiving is more receptive than active, a reflection of the needs of the person being cared for. If the care you give is originating from an active place, it is serving your needs more than the needs of the recipient. Listen and observe. Still your own emotional waters until they can clearly and accurately reflect the subject of your attention, including when that subject is yourself. If you need inspiration, look to the reflected light of Cancer's ruling planet, the Moon.

Pouring your heart out to and into another feels great. Doing it in a way that is safe and supportive for both of you is divine. Protective impulses are heightened under the influence of Cancer. We long to prevent our circle of loved ones from getting hurt, to keep them feeling safe and secure. Be sure to keep yourself in the center of this circle. Just like with the oxygen masks on the plane, you are much better equipped to love others when you love yourself first. Model the care you need to receive by caring for yourself. Those who love you, those who are practicing reflective nurturing, will see clearly and follow your lead. Make sure they are getting the right picture.

Sharing and receiving love is one of the greatest experiences a human can have. Love is magick. Maintaining an open channel for love to flourish takes work and dedication. To become fully immersed in the depths of emotion you've got to maintain a grounded, practical approach to heart maintenance. Check in with friends on a schedule, pour your heart out in a daily

Cancer season is a time to nurture your heart, float your emotions to the surface, and restore your relationship with yourself.

journal, cleanse your crystals under the full moon—any regular practice that keeps you accountable to your own emotional well-being is a great anchor to keep you steady as you open to deep connection with others.

The Sun moves through Cancer just after the summer solstice in the Northern Hemisphere and just after the winter solstice in the Southern Hemisphere (see page 11), one of the two points in the year when day and night are most disparate in length. While the Sun travels through Cancer, open your heart to trust in the universal flow of love.

Cancer in Tarot

Cancer is associated with The Chariot in tarot. The Chariot teaches us to quiet our minds and open our hearts and eyes so that we can recognize our chariot, the one meant to help nurture us and ease our burden when it arrives. It's often much easier to see what type of help would be most beneficial to others, but we can be blind to the same needs in ourselves. Learning to know and accept when you need help is one of the most valuable gifts you can give yourself.

Cancer's ruling planet, the Moon, is associated with The High Priestess, reminding us that strong, healthy boundaries around our sacred spaces are essential to the full expression of Cancerian love.

The Chariot

The High Priestess

Cancer Season Activities

- Writing love letters

- Cooking at home

- Long baths

- Surrounding yourself with rose quartz

- Mutual radical validation parties

- Moon gazing

- Holding hands with friends

- Reading to children and animals

- Donating funds and goods to charity

- Volunteering for a local service organization

Cancer Season Journaling

Get ready to pour your heart out. This season is all about writing love letters—to yourself. Think of all the times in your life when you were in need of some extra TLC, a little cheerleading, a healthy dose of unadulterated admiration. Then, fill that need. How many love letters you write will depend on how many versions of yourself need one. You may have many, many pages to write to yourself at one particular time in the past, or you may need those love letters right here and now. Take time at the beginning of the season to reflect on what your heart, past and present, needs to feel whole and then commit to filling those needs. This simple promise to yourself will be the first of many glowing affirmations you receive.

If this feels overwhelming, start small. Think about what words of kindness or encouragement would make your day easier, write them down, then read them out loud to yourself. Once you are comfortable with this practice, you can begin to add words of admiration and love. Tuning in daily to your emotional needs not only heals in the present, but it also opens channels of communication with the versions of ourselves in the past that did not get the care we needed. These wounded children, teens, young, and not-so-young adults will finally feel safe enough to emerge into your consciousness to receive the love and support they were denied when they needed it.

Cancer Season Tarot

Love is a two-way channel. How we give and receive love are equally important and deeply related. These practices shift depending on who, what, when, and where we are in life and who we are giving and receiving love with. Start by focusing this spread on your love with yourself. Do it once a day for a week before moving on to other relationships with people, organizations, and projects.

1 Your role in the dynamic

2 The role of the other (when focusing this spread on yourself, this will represent the other main aspect of your personality coming to the forefront)

3 How you are currently giving or showing love

4 How you are invited to give or show love

5 How you are receiving love

6 How you are invited to receive love

7 How your giving of love is influencing the relationship

8 How your acceptance of love is influencing the relationship

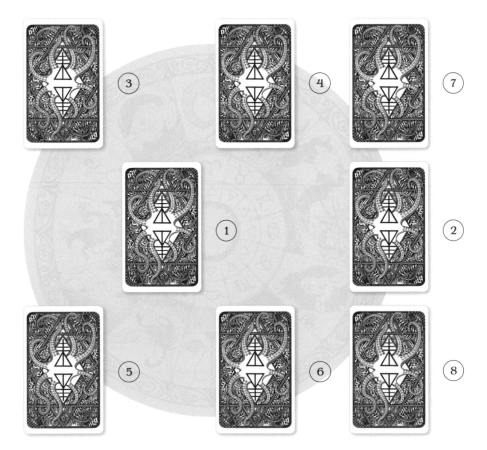

Sample reading

While you are most comfortable riding the emotional waves of life, there is part of you that longs to be part of an established community. Though your ability to set aside time and space for yourself to think and process serves you well, it is time to think outside the box and begin to explore other avenues of self-care. You offer yourself a great deal of compassion and understanding. It is time to allow your passion to be ignited as well. The dedication you have shown to providing solace for yourself has given you a measure of stability and grounding that will be a great support for the opening of your heart to new love and connection.

Cards pulled

1 King of Cups
2 Ten of Coins
3 The Hermit
4 Three of Wands
5 Nine of Cups
6 Knight of Cups
7 Four of Coins
8 Two of Cups

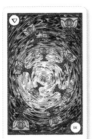

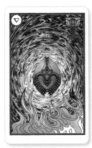

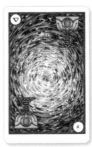

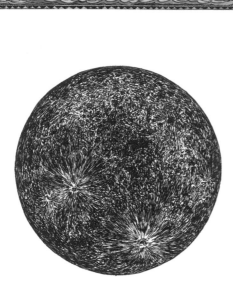

SUN   CANCER   CANCER   MOON

New Moon: Sun in Cancer, Moon in Cancer

The new moon in Cancer is our annual invitation to cleanse our hearts and restore our connection with ourselves, the Divine, and our loved ones.

Wash it all away: any old slights or deep wounds, the emotional debris that collects in the heart channel, the rules of love you lived by yesterday. Let them all float away and forgive yourself if there are any you feel you've held on to for too long. How will your cleansed heart space expand? Who will you invite to take refuge there? What inspiration will you plant? Now is the time to dream big emotionally, forming visions of how you feel in your greatest fantasy future and beginning to pull that future into the present.

The ritual for this new moon is designed to free your heart and open it to a whole new world of emotional possibilities.

New Moon Ritual

Gather what you have of the following:

- Smoke, spray, or bell
- Small dish of water
- Printouts or drawings of the Ace of Cups and the Ace of Coins cards
- Roses and/or fresh rosemary
- Rose quartz, small enough to fit in the dish of water
- Six coins

1 Clear the energy of your space (see page 22), then close your eyes and take three deep, cleansing breaths to ground yourself.

2 Place the dish of water in the center of your altar, the Ace of Cups on the left, and the Ace of Coins on the right.

3 Arrange the roses and/or rosemary around the dish of water.

4 Set the rose quartz where you can reach it easily and hold the coins in your left hand.

5 Close your eyes and allow yourself to settle into your body. When you are ready, envision yourself sinking down from the surface of a warm, gentle sea, past fish and turtles, all animals of the sea, all the way to the bottom. When you get to the bottom, you realize you have been encased in a kind of dried mud that is now loosening and falling away, leaving you clean and refreshed. When all the mud has fallen away, dig into the sea floor and retrieve six golden coins. Check to see if they have any symbols on their surface and make a mental note of any. When you are ready, gently open your eyes.

6 Still holding the coins in your left hand, put the rose quartz in the water.

7 Transfer the coins to your right hand and drop them in the water one by one, feeling your heart strengthen more and more with each drop

8 Leave the dish of water, rose quartz, and coins out under the new moon.

9 When your spell is done, use your love water to water your favorite plant or pour it over your hands for a loving cleanse and be sure to add any symbols you saw on the coins to your ritual notes.

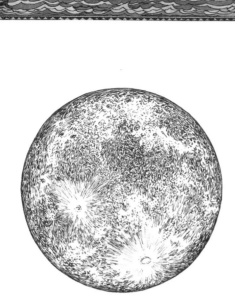

SUN

CANCER | CAPRICORN

MOON

Full Moon: Sun in Cancer, Moon in Capricorn

The full moon of Cancer season is in the opposite sign of Capricorn. The full moon in Capricorn is our annual opportunity to clear out any outdated beliefs or wounds that are keeping us from pursuing our goals.

The Cancer/Capricorn axis teaches us to observe and adjust how we invest our energy and what we gain from that investment. To feel deeply secure requires both emotional and material wellness, yet too often we hyper-focus on one to the detriment of the other. Your heart and your head are not enemies. They are on the same team, working to keep you safe and sound. Pay attention to any fears of lack that come up and take steps to soothe or solve them. Any energy used to shore up your sanctuary is well spent.

The ritual for this full moon is designed to gently illuminate and release limiting beliefs, and fill your heart with divine love and support.

The Devil

The Chariot

Full Moon Ritual

Gather what you have of the following:

- Smoke, spray, or bell
- Small dish of water
- Printouts or drawings of The Devil and The Chariot cards
- Pen
- Black obsidian, small enough to fit in the dish of water, and rose quartz
- Two strawberries

1 Clear the energy of your space (see page 22), then close your eyes and take three deep, cleansing breaths to ground yourself.

2 Place the small dish of water in the center of your altar.

3 On the back of the image of The Devil, write any belief or recurring thought that keeps you from working toward your goals. (If you have trouble thinking of something, ask yourself what your worst critic would say if you told them what you plan to accomplish.)

4 Rip the image of The Devil into small pieces and submerge them in the water, then place the black obsidian on top of them.

5 Cover the dish of water with the image of The Chariot.

6 Hold the rose quartz to your heart and spend a few moments breathing pink light in through the rose quartz and exhaling gray smoke.

7 Place a strawberry in front of the dish as a thanks to the universe and eat one to thank yourself.

8 When you are through performing the ritual, remove the obsidian from the dish and dispose of the water and paper.

♌ Leo Season

JULY 23–AUGUST 22 • FIXED FIRE • I ANNOUNCE...

Leo is symbolized by the lion, glorious ruler of the savannah. Lions are the apex predator of the African continent, making their only potential threat, outside of poachers, other lions. They spend most of their days just lying around, resting, sleeping. During the brief hours they are active, their time is spent hunting, socializing, or patrolling. The instinctual behavior of wild lions translated to the world of humans is easily misread as laziness. Seen another way, lions simply have nothing to prove. They have complete confidence that their strength is known and seen whether they are taking down a zebra or fast asleep in the afternoon sun.

Carrying yourself with pride is about more than feeling good about your accomplishments. True pride comes from a deep inner knowing that you are inherently worthy of appreciation, of admiration, that you matter. Sometimes we mistake pride for arrogance and make ourselves small in order to avoid seeming boastful. Let go of any anxiety about telling the two apart. Boasting comes from a lack of confidence, and is intended to make others feel small in order to make oneself feel larger, or can even be an attempt to fill a hole in the soul with coerced compliments. When you know you have created something compelling, that you have worked hard, that you have done your best, and you want to share that with the world, that is pride. Practice pride liberally and often! It is inspiring and contagious.

When your practice of pride becomes a habit, your presence in the world shifts. When you walk into a room, the energy changes and people respond to you differently. You may notice that your boundaries are respected without even needing to speak them out loud. We often hear about stage presence, the ability of a performer to command attention without saying a word, but the same quality shines forth from people off stage as well, in all walks of life. Your presence is like your personal gravity—it's what draws others into your orbit. Habitual pride ensures others will be drawn to you for what you value in yourself—and reflect back to you how beneficial your presence is in their lives and in the world.

As you move through life, your presence announces to the world who you are and what

Leo season is a time to unleash the power of your presence and the message of your power.

you stand for. It does so wordlessly, yet speaks volumes. You can send powerful messages that reverberate through the world just by being you. How you carry yourself lets others know how you expect to be treated and how they can expect to be treated by you. It can signal to others that it is safe to express who they are and freely communicate their deeply held principles. Just as you would choose your words carefully in crafting a public speech about what means most to you, take the time to ensure the message your presence conveys accurately communicates your hopes, ideals, and beliefs.

While the Sun travels through Leo, be brave, be bold, be yourself, and most of all, be unabashedly proud of who you are.

Leo in Tarot

Leo is associated with the Strength card. Strength is something inherent to our beings. It flows through and emanates from us, whether we are demonstrating it or lying still. Even when you are exhausted, your connection to the Earth and the Universe ensures your true strength will not be diminished. It is the source of power that fuels the light of your presence in the world.

Leo's ruling planet is the Sun and is associated, appropriately, with The Sun. Your vital force is true and plain to see. You do not need to look under any rocks or into dark corners to find it and neither does anyone else.

Leo Season Activities

- Throwing a dinner party

- Attending (or speaking at) a conference

- Starting a book club

- Hosting a clothing exchange

- Celebrating your skills and accomplishments

- Meeting new people

- Soaking in the sun (safely, of course)

- Wearing gold

- Organizing a group outing

- Going big or going home

Leo Season Journaling

To help you refine the message of your presence in the world, you'll be examining the presence of people you admire and what message you receive from their presence. Every week, choose a person you admire. Begin with someone you do not know personally. This will help to separate the public persona from the private person. After the first week, you can consider people you know if you like, or you can stick with people you don't. Feel free to repeat this exercise more than once a week. The only true limit is the number of people you admire.

When you write, answer the following questions:

1 Why do you admire this person?

2 How do you feel when you see them (in person, in print, on screen)?

3 Is there an implicit or explicit message they project?

4 Does this message have an impact on how you see yourself?

5 What does your experience of this person tell you about your own message for the world?

Leo Season Tarot Spread

Get up close and personal with your public self with this tarot spread. Knowing who you are and how you influence others is valuable knowledge. It enables you to make choices about what you can amp up or dial down in certain situations depending on your goals and intentions. What do your manner and behavior announce to the world? To your family? Your friends? Colleagues? You can do this spread once for each "audience" in your life. If there are adjustments you want to make, wait at least a month before repeating for the same group.

1 How you want to be seen

2 How you feel you are seen

3 How those close to you see you

4 How strangers see you

5 What you are invited to let go of and stop projecting

6 What you are invited to project more of

Sample reading

There is a part of you that longs to share difficult emotions, to be seen as someone who isn't afraid to face the wounds of the past. You may feel you are instead seen as someone who simply takes life as it comes, trusting your gut to lead you without stopping to take it all in.

The wisdom you seek to project is seen. Those close to you trust your words and your ability to analyze a situation and strangers admire your ability to accomplish great things through creativity and ingenuity—even magick.

You can move away from restraining yourself. The general moderation you've practiced has served you well, but it is now time to focus it on specific places in your life that need rebalancing. When you bring peace to your own heart through direct action, you'll inspire others to do the same.

Cards pulled

1 Five of Cups

2 Two of Wands

3 Six of Swords

4 Ten of Wands

5 Temperance

6 Justice

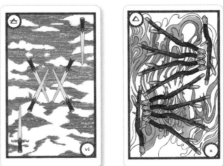

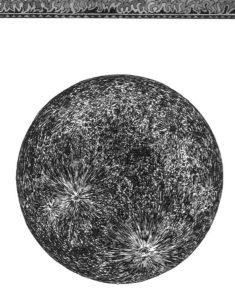

SUN   LEO   LEO   MOON

New Moon: Sun in Leo, Moon in Leo

The new moon in Leo is our annual invitation to shine like the sun in our own personal solar system, proudly and without reservation.

There is no more pretending. Any parts of yourself you've been keeping under wraps are clamoring for attention. You need to be visible, all of you. Your eccentricities paint a beautiful picture of who you are and where you've been. The story of your life told by your language, attitudes, mannerisms, empathy, style, ideals, and all-round way of interacting with others is valuable. Air it all out, polish it up, turn up the volume, and adjust the lighting. The world is your stage. Your fellow performers are waiting to explore the big, wide, wonderful world of humanity with you.

The ritual for this new moon is designed to amplify all the things that make you *you*, so you can see, celebrate, and love yourself fully and then accept that level of love and appreciation from others.

New Moon Ritual

Gather what you have of the following:

- Smoke, spray, or bell
- Yellow seven-day ritual candle
- Piece of paper with your full name and date of birth written on it
- Printouts or drawings of Strength and The Sun cards
- Sunflowers
- Orange calcite

1 Clear the energy of your space (see page 22), then close your eyes and take three deep, cleansing breaths to ground yourself.

2 Place the candle in the center of your altar area on top of the paper with your name and date of birth on it, then place the image of Strength on the left and the image of The Sun on the right.

3 Arrange the sunflowers in a circle around the candle (you can break off the stems so you just have the flowers).

4 Hold the orange calcite in your hand as you light the candle and say,

"I step out into the sun, completely exposed, completely loved."

5 Still holding the crystal in your hand, close your eyes and spend a few minutes settling into your body. Picture yourself in an open desert under the noon sun. There is no shade, and no signs of life of any kind as far as you can see, yet somehow you do not feel afraid. The heat of the sun is filling you with liquid gold and it nourishes every part of your being. Once you are completely filled with gold, spend a few moments glowing in the desert, then gently open your eyes.

6 Let the candle burn until it goes out on its own (see page 23), then discard the flowers.

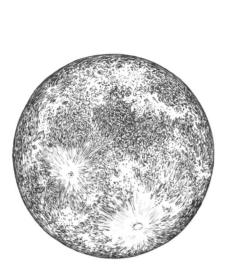

SUN   LEO | AQUARIUS   MOON

Full Moon: Sun in Leo, Moon in Aquarius

The full moon of Leo season is in the opposite sign of Aquarius. The full moon in Aquarius is our annual opportunity to come to embrace both our dependence on and separation from our community.

The Leo/Aquarius axis shows us how the individual and collective selves depend on each other to exist as separate but deeply interrelated identities. We all stand not only on the shoulders of giants, but also arm in arm with those we surround ourselves with. This connection does not make us less unique. Our communities are an extension of ourselves and an aspect of our individuality. And the particular history and personality we bring to the group make it richer and stronger. Acknowledging this inherent connection is the essence of the humanitarian impulse. What unique trait facilitates your connection with others? How does your outward persona reflect the humanitarian values of your group?

The ritual for this full moon is designed to help you transcend any false separations between you and others so you can fully embrace your role in collective evolution.

Full Moon Ritual

Gather what you have of the following:

- Smoke, spray, or bell
- Candle holder or small plate
- Lemurian seed quartz crystal, fluorite, and blue kyanite
- Printouts or drawings of The Star and Ten of Coins cards
- Small nail
- Paper and pen
- White or pale blue taper candle
- Ten coins

1 Clear the energy of your space (see page 22), then close your eyes and take three deep, cleansing breaths to ground yourself.

2 Set your altar as follows:

Center: small plate or candle holder with Lemurian seed quartz in front
Left: image of The Star with blue kyanite on top
Right: image of the Ten of Coins with fluorite on top

3 Using the small nail, carve into the candle the words:

"We are one, we are safe, we are abundant."

4 On the paper, write down ten things that are essential for a healthy, thriving community. Try to list at least one thing each from the physical, emotional, intellectual, and spiritual realms.

5 Place the candle in the candle holder or melt the bottom slightly and stick it to the plate, then light the candle.

6 Read the ten items on your list aloud, and as you do, place one of the coins on the image of the Ten of Coins for each item.

7 Let the candle burn until it goes out on its own (see page 23), then discard the wax and bury the ten coins near your home.

♍ Virgo Season

VIRGO

MUTABLE

EARTH

AUGUST 23–SEPTEMBER 22 • MUTABLE EARTH • I MUST...

Virgo is symbolized by the maiden, the temple keeper, unattached to a domestic life, spiritually pure. The life of the maiden is meticulous by necessity. Care must be taken to keep the temple fires burning, the veneration of the deities performed to their expectations and standards. The well-being of the entire community depends on the adept performance of these rites. The maiden is chosen for this role by divine decree, born into a life of service. This is not a burden, but an honor.

Meticulous attention to detail and exacting standards are the backbone of magickal practices and religious rites all over the world. Specific offerings must be made, words uttered in a set order, all movements performed just as they always have been. These details are loaded with meaning. The ways in which we perform the rituals of our earthly lives are also full of meaning, meaning we are often unaware of. Examine the details in your actions, especially those which seem the most mundane. Does sweeping the floor in a specific way feel like you're under the watchful eye of a critical parent, or a doting grandparent? Does the food you make available for yourself reflect how you feel about yourself or how someone else feels about you? Noticing these subtleties, without judgment, is the first step in living full time as the divine creature you are.

The way your home is organized also speaks silent volumes about what is most important to you. If you want to do more yoga, it helps a lot to have your yoga mat readily available. The same principle applies to every aspect of your life. Arrange your closet so the clothes that make you feel radiant are most accessible and see how much more you wear them as a result. Are your books put away in a cupboard or displayed out in the open? Which ones are easiest to reach? It will take time and effort to organize your space to support your priorities— and it will be worth every minute. Our physical surroundings are a mirror of our interior state and vice versa. Choosing a life of prioritizing what is personally sacred to you and fine-tuning your life to reflect and support that is a very powerful act of self-love and respect.

Virgo season is a time to recognize the divine nature of earthly tasks and to prioritize all that is sacred to you.

Everyone's version of sacred is a little different. Our life experiences and individual makeup mean that the exact same actions can have vastly divergent impacts on our lives. Organizing one's life around exercise or healthy eating may be a beautiful way to honor the body for one person and a dangerous trigger for body dysmorphia for another. Your sacred life is yours to define and redefine. While your priorities in life may change, you can always choose to center what is most sacred to you in the present. Your body is the temple of your spirit, your home the temple of your life on Earth. Keep your flames burning bright, wherever and whenever you are in your life.

While the Sun travels through Virgo, raise your standards to meet your ideals while remaining compassionate and accepting of those of others.

Virgo in Tarot

Virgo is associated with The Hermit, devoted loner of the tarot, choosing solitude to concentrate their efforts more thoroughly on gathering and synthesizing wisdom. While The Hermit may seem a bit self-absorbed to some, this strict adherence to the work and the boundaries it requires is actually serving a lofty altruistic purpose—bringing the product of this work back out to the world in the form of guidance. The Hermit's lantern shines in the dark, leading others on the spiritual path.

Virgo's ruling planet, Mercury, is associated with The Magician, assuring that the grounded, practical means will always be helped along to magickal end.

The Hermit

The Magician

Virgo Season Activities

- Deep cleaning (of home, office, or studio)
- Enjoying time alone
- Setting a sacred space
- Communing with nature
- Self-directed studying
- Prioritizing wellness

- Updating skin and body care rituals
- Crystal gridding your home
- Honoring your inner priestess
- Expanding your loungewear collection
- One-on-one time with friends who inspire you

Virgo Season Journaling

There are many ways to complete a task. Finding the one that feels both effortless and meaningful for you is the key to sticking to any goal or practice long term. To help you discover what works best for you, we'll begin with a fact-finding mission.

For one week, record everything you do every day. You can simplify this by making three columns on a page: task, time started, and time completed. Start a new page each day. Include everything and be as specific as possible. You may be surprised by how much or how little time you spend on certain things.

At the end of the week, go through your data with three highlighters in green, yellow, and orange or pink, and mark each task according to your experience. Mark things you enjoy in green, things you are neutral about in yellow, and things you do not enjoy in orange or pink. Notice if there are any patterns.

Now that you've got some insight into how your days are spent, you can make informed choices about your time. Perhaps orange tasks can be grouped together to get them all done at once. You may prefer to take more time with green tasks or to stretch them out over multiple days. Turn yellow tasks green with simple tweaks. Make some decisions, then plot out your next week and follow the new schedule very strictly.

During your scheduled week, write a page every day about how you feel—emotionally, physically, mentally, spiritually. You don't have to analyze, just take notes. For the remaining two weeks, continue to note how you feel every day and to make conscious adjustments to your schedule of tasks. By the end of this season, you should be skilled in making the work you do work for you.

Virgo Season Tarot

While it can be easy to identify what we feel devoted to, knowing what to do with that devotion can be less clear—and it changes day by day. Use this spread whenever you need clarity on how to express your devotion, up to once a day. As you use it, you'll begin to see patterns that can help you to know yourself and understand your spirituality more deeply.

1 How to express your devotion

2 Where/how you can receive support

3 What effect this has on you

Sample reading

Take time to explore the world deep within, past the concerns of your daily life, past surface memories, way down to your greatest hopes and fears, where fundamental beliefs reside. These trips down into your psyche are offerings, the information you gather is sacred. It can feel selfish to be so focused on the self, but this is your gift to the Divine.

Find comfort and restoration in creative expression. Follow your heart. Coloring books will work just as well as oil paints. Whatever creative activity makes your heart feel full will help to cleanse any old emotional residue that may get dredged up.

This work is leading you to a greater peace and expansion. Your understanding of the pace and rhythm of the Universe is deepening, as is, most importantly, your acceptance of its timing and the luck it brings.

There are unseen forces looking out for you and looking on as you commit to your devotional practice.

Cards pulled

1 The Moon

2 Queen of Wands

3 The Wheel of Fortune

The Moon

The Wheel of Fortune

SUN   VIRGO   VIRGO   MOON

New Moon: Sun in Virgo, Moon in Virgo

The new moon in Virgo is our annual invitation to clean house—physically, energetically, spiritually— and reinvigorate our habits with purpose.

Attention to detail, adherence to systems and schedules, and high standards are commonly associated with work and career. But you know what else they're great for? A stunningly beautiful and powerful spiritual practice. Breathe fresh life into your rituals, magickal and mundane, and walk away from any that have outlived their purpose. You are not bound by the pattern of the past. The future awaits your vision and direction to take form as you build it, day by day.

The ritual for this new moon is designed to help you see and experience all aspects of your life as expressions of your divine nature.

New Moon Ritual

Gather what you have of the following:

- **Smoke, spray, or bell**
- **Printouts or drawings of The Hermit and Ace of Coins cards**
- **Pen**
- **White seven-day ritual candle**
- **Jasmine oil and pure licorice root tea**
- **Sodalite**

1 Clear the energy of your space (see page 22), then close your eyes and take three deep, cleansing breaths to ground yourself.

2 On the back of the image of The Hermit, write three aspects of your spiritual beliefs that are important for you to connect with every day—for example, acceptance, love, forgiveness, release, gratitude, connection, humility, or love.

3 On the back of the image of the Ace of Coins, write three tools you have to connect with your spirituality, divine self, and/or the Universe that you can use daily—for example, meditation, altar tending, prayer, chanting, anointing and/or adorning your body, or lighting incense or candles.

4 Place the candle in the center of your altar area with The Hermit on the left and the Ace of Coins on the right.

5 Put a drop of jasmine oil on top of the candle and trace it around three times clockwise, then sprinkle a tiny bit of licorice root on top.

6 Light the candle and say,

"My spiritual ideals are reflected in my daily life and are ever evolving under the guidance of the Universe."

7 Spend a few minutes visualizing yourself going through a day, performing all your spiritual rituals, feeling your divine and earthly lives as one. Try to be as detailed as possible and see yourself through the whole day, from the time you wake up until you fall asleep.

8 Let the candle burn until it goes out on its own (see page 23).

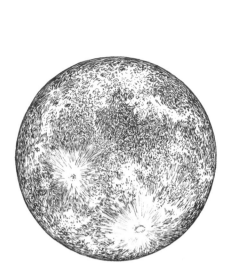

SUN VIRGO | PISCES MOON

Full Moon: Sun in Virgo, Moon in Pisces

The full moon of Virgo season is in the opposite sign of Pisces. The full moon in Pisces is our annual opportunity to open our eyes to the evidence of our own magickal powers all around us.

The Virgo/Pisces axis asks us to accept the pragmatic and the fantastical as equally valuable ways of understanding the world around us. Dreams are documentation of truth. Empirical evidence of the storage capacity of quartz crystals affirms their magickal use as holders of divine teachings. There is magick in talismans, divination, and spells, and also in a flower blooming, kindness between strangers, and snow falling on a clear day. Mystical expression in all its forms is illuminated by this moon and we are called to find value and meaning in each of them.

The ritual for this full moon is designed to awaken, activate, and amplify the elemental magick living inside you.

Full Moon Ritual

Gather what you have of the following:

- Smoke, spray, or bell
- Printouts or drawings of The Moon and The Magician cards
- Whole nutmeg and cinnamon stick
- Feather, chalice or small dish of water, small twig, and coin
- Tea candle
- Labradorite

1 Clear the energy of your space (see page 22), then close your eyes and take three deep, cleansing breaths to ground yourself.

2 Place the tarot images side by side in the center of your altar, with The Moon on the left and The Magician on the right.

3 Set the nutmeg on The Moon and the cinnamon stick on The Magician.

4 Arrange the feather, chalice, twig, and coin in a line in that order from left to right in front of the images.

5 Light the candle, then hold the labradorite in your hands and spend a few moments gazing at each of your elemental symbols, opening yourself up to the powers of each one and thanking them for being with you. The feather lights up your Air center, your head and throat, home of intellect and communication. The chalice lights up your Water center, your heart, home of emotion. The twig (wand) lights up your Fire center, your lower abdomen, home of instinct, action, creativity, and magick. The coin lights up your Earth center, the bottom of your feet, home of your connection with the ground.

6 Set the labradorite in the center front of your altar and let the candle burn out on its own (see page 23).

LIBRA

CARDINAL

AIR

Libra Season

SEPTEMBER 23–OCTOBER 22 • CARDINAL AIR • I BALANCE...

Libra is symbolized by the scales, emblem of justice, fairness, and equality. While this is the only symbol of the zodiac that is an inanimate object, the scales of Libra have been related to animate representations of justice throughout recorded history, such as Egyptian god Anubis, weighing the hearts of the deceased against a feather to determine their worthiness in the afterlife, and the Greek personification of law, Themis.

Equilibrium is an ongoing process, not a static state. True balance requires constant motion, patience, and great power. The Earth moves all year to bring us to our two equinoxes. The core strength and continual movement required of the human body to balance on uneven ground teach us how much emotional fortitude and dexterity we are using to remain even-keeled in stressful situations. It's not only okay to perpetually adjust your balance, it's desirable. Getting comfortable with the sway of your own ship in the waves will help you to find true fairness in every situation and stay away from forming rigid rules that pull you off your center and create walls between you and others.

The urge for balance is not only about fairness; it is about the beauty of harmony between people. Finding the right vibration is a gift, maintaining it is an art. If there are

relationships in your life that are in turmoil or even just a little uncomfortable, assess the situation and address it or disengage. No need for dramatic confrontations. If you need to walk away at this time, simply walk away. Take some space. Bridge burning is not worth the energy. Save that effort for yourself. Your inner peace is central to maintaining a healthy relationship with others. Care for yourself as you would a beloved friend or partner. Give yourself assurance, encouragement, and plenty of rest and compliments.

Speaking of compliments—you're beautiful! Find it, see it, say it, believe it. Refine your aesthetic to align with your values and it becomes impossible to view a love of beauty as frivolous. Remind yourself not only of sights, but sounds, smells, and feelings you find pleasing. Wear clothes that make you feel great. If you

Libra season is a time to find harmony in differences and bring your life into beautiful balance.

don't have any, get some—making sure to find pieces that are made and sold to your ethical standards. Go through your personal care products. Does your shampoo make your hair smell beautiful? Is your skin care producing the results you desire? Personal care rituals are sacred. Be sure you are anointing your body as the divine vessel it is.

The Sun moves through Libra just after the autumnal equinox in the Northern Hemisphere and just after the vernal equinox in the Southern Hemisphere (see page 11), one of the two points in the year when day and night are equal. While the Sun travels through Libra, rediscover your inner and outer radiant beauty and share it with those you hold dear.

Libra in Tarot

Libra is associated with the Justice card in tarot. Justice asks us to look for areas in our lives that are out of balance and to take steps to correct the discord. This can be deeply esoteric and spiritual or straightforward and mundane. When looking for places in need of evening out, start with the most obvious and work your way in.

Libra's ruling planet, Venus, is associated with The Empress. A life of love and abundance promised by The Empress expands the balance of Justice into harmony and beauty.

Justice

The Empress

Libra Season Activities

- Romantic dates

- Reconnecting with old friends

- Spa days (massage, skin care, deep relaxation)

- Wardrobe updates

- Finding the perfect shade of rouge

- Forgiving and forgetting

- Attending social gatherings—bonus points for parties that call for elegant attire

- Standing up for a loved one

- Bringing awareness to an injustice

Libra Season Journaling

Internal vs. external, science vs. magick, me vs. them. These dichotomies break down when we look at them closely, as do most. On a molecular level, there is no rigid delineation between internal and external; the tiny particles of our bodies just fade out into the air. Many practices once viewed as scientific would now seem like magickal thinking at best and science continues to reach into magickal realms (the recent surge of Western medical interest in the healing potential of traditional psychedelic medicines, for example). And the personal and the collective are constantly enmeshed.

Every week, choose a different pair of opposites to explore. You've got three you can use in that last paragraph already! Start the week by drawing a line down the middle of

your paper, writing one opposite at the top of each column, and filling the columns with a list of attributes of their respective subject. Try to fill the page. Repeat this practice the next day with the same set of opposites and no repetitions from the first day (things will start to get weird—weird is good). For the remaining days, choose one attribute from each column and write for ten minutes about how these attributes are different and then for ten minutes about how they are the same or similar.

This practice will help to soften the rigid boundaries of categorization in your mind and allow you to see that you don't have to work so hard at evening things out or ensuring fairness. The Universe has done a pretty great job of it already.

Libra Season Tarot

Explore the relationship between you and another person or situation. The left side of the spread shows how the situation is developing while the right sheds light on your personal role in the dynamic. Try looking at the two sides of the spread as cohesive units, then see how they feel next to each other and what they bring to mind for you. How do they fit together? Do they seem to attract or repel each other?

1 The nature of the situation

2 What has grown from it

3 The direction of future growth

4 Your role in the situation

5 What your role is grounded in

6 How you are invited to move forward

Sample reading

This situation has great potential for grounded success. It has sparked intense passion that will fuel forward momentum and an open, creative atmosphere. Harness the magick of this creative thinking to ensure long-term stability.

You offer a large amount of practical wisdom to this situation. At the same time, your participation in this dynamic offers you opportunities for building new skills. This is a major turning point for you, something that is changing your life as you know it. Don't be afraid to shed old habits.

Your practical skills are becoming more flexible, more fluid. Follow your gut and visualize big things. Your magick is growing.

Cards pulled

1 Six of Coins

2 Knight of Wands

3 Eight of Coins

4 Nine of Coins

5 The World

6 Nine of Wands

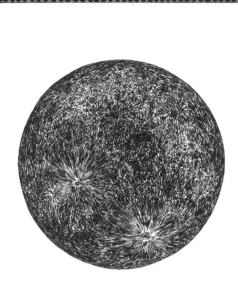

SUN   LIBRA   LIBRA   MOON

New Moon: Sun in Libra, Moon in Libra

The new moon in Libra is our annual invitation to zero out our relational ledger and restart our personal connections with a clean slate.

Sometimes the Libran impulse to balance gets a little... impulsive. Balancing can turn into score keeping which can lead to resentment. Let it all go and start fresh. Forget who bought lunch last, whether you've called your friend to check in more or vice versa, who brought the best bottle of wine to the dinner party. It doesn't matter. What matters is you maintaining your own equilibrium by setting boundaries with your energy and sticking to them. Lighten your heart and clear your mind. You've got your whole gorgeous life ahead of you. Enjoy it.

The ritual for this new moon is designed to lift the weight of the world off your internal scales, leaving you cool, calm, collected, and ready to move forward with clear vision and an open heart.

New Moon Ritual

Gather what you have of the following:

- Smoke, spray, or bell
- Printout or drawing of the Justice card
- Tea candle
- Fluorite (any color) and peacock ore
- Olive oil and fresh dill

1 Clear the energy of your space (see page 22), then close your eyes and take three deep, cleansing breaths to ground yourself.

2 Place the Justice image in the center of your altar.

3 Set the tea candle on top of the Justice image, the fluorite on the left, and the peacock ore on the right.

4 Trace a drop of olive oil around the top of the candle three times clockwise.

5 Rub the dill between your hands, then place it in front of the candle.

6 Bring your hands up to your face and inhale deeply, then light the candle and say,

"My heart is as light as a feather, my vision is clear, my voice is true."

7 Close your eyes and take a deep inhale, visualizing bright, sparking light filling your entire body. On your exhale, release any remaining debris that once clouded your perception.

8 Gently open your eyes and thank the Universe, your guides and angels, the Divine—however you frame it/them.

9 Let the candle burn until it goes out on its own (see page 23).

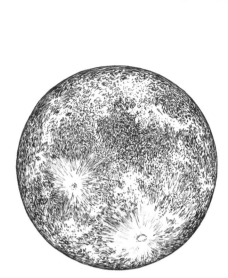

SUN · LIBRA | ARIES · MOON

Full Moon: Sun in Libra, Moon in Aries

The full moon of Libra season is in the opposite sign of Aries. The full moon in Aries is our annual opportunity to shed identities that no longer fit.

The axis of Libra/Aries highlights how we see ourselves as individuals versus how we see ourselves in relation to others. Our self-image is formed over time, starting with our role in our family of origin and constantly evolving as we develop and experience new things and people. Sometimes old fragments of our identity stick long after we've outgrown them. You are free to reject any labels that are not in alignment with your emotional and spiritual growth and health.

The ritual for this full moon is designed to empower you to be radically yourself and trust that the more YOU you are, the stronger your core relationships will be.

Full Moon Ritual

Gather what you have of the following:

- Smoke, spray, or bell
- Printouts or drawings of the Ace of Wands and the Ace of Swords cards
- Tea candle
- Incense (preferably cedarwood) and incense burner or holder
- Pyrite and labradorite

1 Clear the energy of your space (see page 22), then close your eyes and take three deep, cleansing breaths to ground yourself.

2 Place the Ace of Wands image on the left side of your altar, Ace of Swords to the right. Then place the tea candle on the Ace of Wands image and the incense holder and incense on the Ace of Swords image. Hold both crystals in your left hand.

3 Light the candle and then say,

"Elemental Fire, ignite the parts of me most needed for the next phase and burn away any that are no longer needed."

4 Light the incense and say,

"Elemental Air, give me clear vision to see my unique strengths and the discernment to know when to use them; take any thoughts or words that are not serving me as easily as smoke blowing away in the wind."

5 Take one deep inhale, taking in the wisdom of elemental Fire and Air, then exhale anything impeding their message. Then say,

"I am whole, I am valuable, I am enough."

6 Take a few moments to let the magick integrate, then thank the Universe, your guides and angels, the Divine—however you frame it/them.

7 Place the crystals between the two images and let the candle burn until it goes out on its own (see page 23).

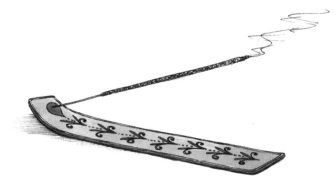

LIBRA SEASON

SCORPIO

FIXED

▽

WATER

Scorpio Season

OCTOBER 23 - NOVEMBER 21 • FIXED WATER • I RELEASE / I EMBRACE...

Scorpio has two symbolic animal associations: the scorpion and the eagle. Though scorpions live in dry environments, the deep psychological impact they carry— being potentially deadly, small, and hiding in shadowy corners—provokes strong emotions and secures their status as the darkest of the Water signs. When we are disturbed in the private recesses of our emotions, like the scorpion, we tend to sting. The eagle is a less commonly known but equally powerful symbol of Scorpio. The ability of eagles to laser-focus on a tiny target reflects the scorpionic power to see with perfect clarity the true center of a situation, the hidden motivations behind seemingly bizarre behavior.

Diving deep into your psyche is encouraged in some form throughout the year, but in Scorpio season it has a different purpose and intensity. Choosing to face fears, old wounds, childhood traumas, and potentially painful truths requires bravery, a robust emotional support system, and a plan to come back up to the surface. Let a trusted friend in on your plans so you've got someone to call on if things get sticky (a good practice for any journey into the unknown). This is a time for supported exploration of your most deeply held emotional attachments and triggers. Treat yourself as you would a scared animal. Be gentle and kind, no sudden movements, and practice loving understanding if you lash out.

This daring adventure into the darkness has a purpose—radical acceptance. Finding the wounded child or embarrassed outcast within and embracing them is one of the most powerful acts of love we can give ourselves. As we grow up, previous versions of ourselves are left behind and we move on. But being outgrown and being resolved are very different things. Retrieving these previous selves and making peace with them allows us to truly evolve as we grow. The simple act of kindness we needed and were denied can be given now. It is never too late. Every part of you is worthy of love. Every. Part.

Release the pain and shame from the past that continue to haunt the present. Reach down into the most hidden parts of your soul and

Scorpio season is a time to embrace your darkest depths and shed shame and extra baggage.

retrieve an emblem of what you have survived and how you have thrived in its wake. Wear it proudly. When you embrace your truth and release shame and judgment, you will glow with love. That glow is a beacon for others who have overcome their own adversity. We shine brightest when we've dared to venture deep into the darkness.

If you have a history of trauma or are going through a particularly difficult time, consult with your therapist or counselor before engaging in the work for Scorpio season. Though all rituals and activities are designed to bring up only what you are prepared to handle, it's best to be sure. Your emotional and psychological well-being are the top priority.

While the Sun travels through Scorpio, take a deep breath and plunge into healing transformation.

Scorpio in Tarot

Scorpio is associated with the Death card in tarot, feared and misunderstood, yet truly one of the most welcome visitors of the deck. Death offers us transformation through release and rebirth, the promise of new life after death. Letting go—of the past, rigid rules in the present, fantasies and projections about the future—frees us to embrace ourselves as we are and to grow organically wherever we are.

Pluto is the ruling planet of Scorpio. Pluto, as the outermost planet, connects us psychically to realms beyond the three-dimensional world we inhabit. It is associated with the Judgment card in tarot, urging us to actively dig deep beneath the surface to uncover both the toxins and the treasure, so we can sort them out and decide what to keep and what to discard.

Scorpio Season Activities

- Writing poetry
- Clearing out clutter and clothes you no longer wear
- Gifting yourself a trinket you always wanted as a kid
- Embracing your dark side
- Watching scary movies
- Starting therapy
- Forgiving yourself
- Painting your fingernails black
- Expressing passions ... physically

Scorpio Season Journaling

The deep psychology of Scorpio lends a mythological air to the season and to our explorations of ourselves. There is an opportunity to see trials and challenges of your past through this lens to find both the lessons gained and the heroic feats you accomplished to earn them. See what wants to come to the surface with this journaling ritual and follow the thread.

Find a time and place where you will not be disturbed. Light a candle or some incense, preferably myrrh. Myrrh has thousands of years of history as a vehicle for crossing the veil between the seen and unseen worlds. Brew a cup of jasmine tea for an additional boost of lunar powers of reflection. Close your eyes and take three deep, cleansing breaths. Then begin, starting with the prompt, "Once upon a time..."

See if you can let a fairy tale flow from your pen onto the page. Don't worry if it doesn't seem to make sense or if it's a retelling of an existing tale. Think of this as a channeled story coming through from your subconscious or higher self. Would you edit or judge your subconscious or higher self? Didn't think so. Let it flow.

Repeat this practice as often as you can—ideally daily, but do what works for you. At the end of the season, look back through your writings and see if you can find a trail of breadcrumbs anywhere, little clues to help you find your way home.

Scorpio Season Tarot Spread

Explore what's going on under the surface of situations or relationships, to gain a deeper understanding of yourself in relation to the outside world—or for inspiration for your fairy tale.

First, choose a card to represent yourself. If you want insight into yourself as a source of abundance, choose The Empress; as a master manifester, The Magician; and so on. Select the rest of the cards as you would for any other tarot spread.

Consider the cards in Positions 2–4 as a unit. When you look at them together, what feeling does it give you? Are they all one suit? Do they agree or conflict? If these cards were people, would they get along at a party or avoid each other?

1 You

2 Forces at play under the surface

3 Forces at play under the surface

4 Forces at play under the surface

5 Integrated lessons

6 Next steps

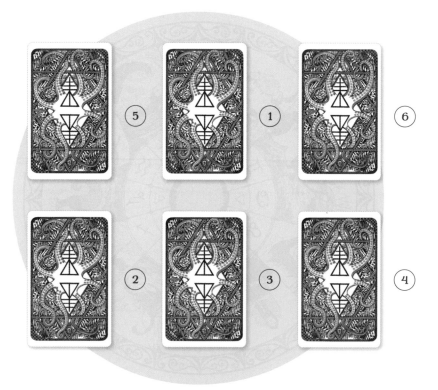

Sample reading

The Devil was chosen to represent feeling stuck, unable to move forward in life, the view of a path forward blocked or obscured. Underneath this veil of confusion are some surprisingly supportive energies that shed light on the block. There is a great need to stop doubting yourself. Your gut instinct and your heart are trying to show you that you are capable of so much more than you think. Accept their messages. You don't need to know exactly how to get where you're going. You only need to know the destination and you will find your way there.

You have become very comfortable speaking your mind and standing up for what you believe in. Now it is time for these beliefs to settle into a world view that will carry you from here to your destination and beyond. Pull back from trying so hard and allow space to receive.

Cards pulled

1 The Devil

2 Seven of Wands

3 Eight of Cups

4 King of Wands

5 Knight of Swords

6 Eight of Swords

SUN   SCORPIO | SCORPIO   MOON

New Moon: Sun in Scorpio, Moon in Scorpio

The new moon in Scorpio is our annual invitation to step through a portal of psychic death and rebirth. Release is usually reserved for the full moons, but with the sign of Scorpio so deeply entrenched in the cycle of life and death, we get an extra dose at this new moon. We are called to bring revolution to the deepest parts of our psyches, clearing the path for the new day ahead. Dare to leave the parts of yourself behind that you've held on to because you think they will please family and friends. Dare to embrace the parts of yourself others have tried to shame you into hiding or abandoning. You can be exactly you. Step out of your old skin and see what has been underneath, waiting to shine.

The ritual for this new moon is designed to empower you to abandon internalized rules and let your freak flag fly.

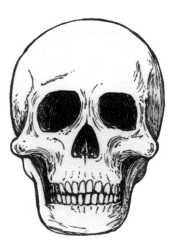

New Moon Ritual

Gather what you have of the following:

- Smoke, spray, or bell
- Printouts or drawings of the Death card or a representation of Death, such as a figurine of a skull or skeleton
- Two small sealed jars of water
- Two tea candles
- Three pieces of black obsidian or black tourmaline
- Green calcite, citrine, and rhodochrosite

1 Clear the energy of your space (see page 22), then close your eyes and take three deep, cleansing breaths to ground yourself.

2 Place the Death image or figure in the center of your altar.

3 Set one jar of water, one tea candle, and the black crystals on the left and the other jar, candle, and crystals on the right.

4 Take the jar on the left in your hands. Close your eyes and visualize energy running through your body, collecting anything that doesn't belong there, and carrying it out of your body and into the jar of water. Continue until you feel "done" (or, alternatively, set a timer for three minutes).

5 Place the jar back on the left, arrange the black crystals around it, and set a tea candle on top of the lid. Then, light the candle.

6 Take one deep, cleansing breath, then take the jar on the right in your hands. Close your eyes and invite your truest self, the self you are stepping into, to awaken. Take your time and see how many details you can make out: feelings, thoughts, attitudes, style, jewelry, hair, musical taste, eating habits—as much as you can gather. Invite all of these wonderful traits to flow through your hands and into the jar.

7 Place the jar back on the right, arrange the remaining crystals around it, and set a tea candle on top of the lid. Then light the candle.

8 While the tea candles burn, try to engage in an activity that you love. Read, play music, write, cook, nap, go for a run—whatever is your happy place is perfect.

9 When the candles have burned out (see page 23), take the jar on the left away from the property you live on and pour out the water. Then come back and drink the water from the jar on the right.

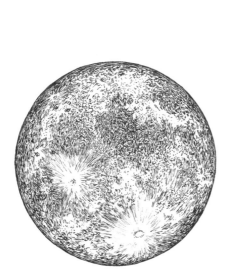

SUN   SCORPIO | TAURUS   MOON

Full Moon: Sun in Scorpio, Moon in Taurus

The full moon of Scorpio season is in the opposite sign of Taurus. The full moon in Taurus is our annual opportunity to examine the habits and structures we are dedicated to and see what is ready to be updated or retired.

The Scorpio/Taurus axis encourages exploration of the bright and dark sides of ritual, ceremony, and routine. Adherence to practice can be profoundly stabilizing or devastatingly limiting. We are called to loosen our grip on tradition for tradition's sake and see which practices and beliefs are working for us and which are working against us. Where are you clinging to old ways out of fear or habit? Are there structures that once served as fortresses that you've since outgrown? What makes up the bare skeleton of your life? How will you build it up again moving forward to support your highest ideals?

The ritual for this full moon is designed to help you gently clear away limiting structures so you can move forward to build new ones in better alignment with your current goals.

Full Moon Ritual

Gather what you have of the following:

- Smoke, spray, or bell
- Printouts or drawings of the Death and The Hierophant cards
- Small dish of water
- Selenite, quartz crystal, and red garnet
- Sesame oil and frankincense oil
- Black seven-day ritual candle

1 Clear the energy of your space (see page 22), then close your eyes and take three deep, cleansing breaths to ground yourself.

2 Place the image of Death in the rear center of your altar with the candle on top, the dish of water in front of that, and the image of The Hierophant in front of the dish.

3 Form an upside-down triangle (the alchemical symbol for Water) on the image of The Hierophant with the crystals, with the red garnet at the point closest to you.

4 Pour a few drops of sesame oil into the dish of water.

5 Anoint yourself with the frankincense oil by touching it to the middle of your forehead, then your heart, and finally the center of the top of your head.

6 Light the candle and spend a few minutes in stillness, gently breathing and inviting the spell to work with your guides and higher self.

7 Let the candle burn until it goes out on its own (see page 23).

SAGITTARIUS

MUTABLE

△

FIRE

Sagittarius Season

NOVEMBER 22–DECEMBER 21 • MUTABLE FIRE • I AIM...

Sagittarius is symbolized by the centaurian archer. Centaurs are plentiful in Greek mythology, but the one associated with Sagittarius is Chiron, the wise, wounded healer who also lends his name and story to an asteroid that plays heavily into many astrological chart interpretations. Chiron's mastery of archery depends on keen vision, sharp reflexes, and exacting aim—skills similarly well-suited for finding the valuable wisdom so often hidden in tragedy and heartbreak.

The literal sharp vision of the archer serves as a metaphor for the visionary vibe inspired by Sagittarius. Lift your head and send your gaze up into the clouds and out beyond the horizon. Take in the vast expanse of possibility that exists in the world and then consider how limited your view still is and how much more exists beyond these limits. Having a vision requires not only seeing over and beyond obstacles, but being able to see the seeds in your life and know what kind of plants they will grow to be. With this knowledge, the skills, gifts, natural talent, relationships, experience, and desire you need to create the life you want can all come together to work toward a common purpose.

There is an art to maintaining focus without sacrificing awareness or care of other projects or personal domains. Variety is the spice of life.

Switch up how you approach working toward your vision from time to time. Depending on who you are, this might mean dividing your day into sections or working diligently at one aspect for days, weeks, or even months before changing up your process. Allow time for rest and leisure. Attentiveness slips into fixation and obsession when not broken up. Let yourself follow your curiosity and wander away once in a while, but make sure you have a plan to come back. Maintaining long-term focus depends on monitoring your peripheral vision and keeping your spirits up.

Optimism is often mistaken for naivety, but the two are worlds apart. Naivety thrives in an absence of information. Optimism sees all of the information clearly, accepts it for what it is, and chooses to see the possibilities through the

Sagittarius season is a time to seek out the silver lining of your dark clouds and shoot for the stars.

limitations. Reject the false choice between being an optimist and a realist. Seeing the bright side is realistic. Knowing what is possible inherently gives you information on what is not. Dreaming big and aiming high do not set you up for disappointment; only expecting a certain outcome when you have no control over it can do that. Open your mind and your heart wide and see just how much they can hold when they are asked to support hopes and not fears.

While the Sun travels through Sagittarius, expand your vision of what is possible.

Sagittarius in Tarot

Sagittarius is associated with the Temperance card in tarot, champion of the virtue of moderation. This may seem an odd fit for fun-loving Sagittarius, until we look more deeply into the card. Temperance doesn't extol moderation for its own sake, but rather as a means to an end. When we stop pouring our energy out without thinking and instead draw it in and conserve our stores, we are free to make choices about where and how we spend it.

Sagittarius' ruling planet, Jupiter, planet of luck and expansion, is associated with The Wheel of Fortune, reminding us that everything unfolds in perfect time with the Universe.

Temperance

The Wheel of Fortune

Sagittarius Season Activities

- Weekend escapes to new places
- Forming a business plan
- Hiking—the more adventurous the better
- Sparkling conversation over sparkling beverages

- Watching travel documentaries
- Learning a new language
- Comedy improv
- Charades
- Archery!

Sagittarius Season Journaling

Use the undying optimism and precision aim of the archer to ignite lofty but specific visions of your future. Choose an area of life to focus on (such as career, home, romance, or family). Make a list of all the goals you have for that part of your life. Write for 20 minutes without stopping—let them all pour out. Pick one goal that is specific, measurable, and maybe sounds a little bit crazy, then go through three steps:

1 Write three additional versions of this goal, each one more ambitious than the last (hey, doesn't that first one seem reasonable and achievable now?).

2 Make a list of everything—EVERY thing—that would bring you close to your goal. Time, money, resources, eating habits, books, podcasts, advice from friends and colleagues, bedding that would help you sleep more soundly, crystals, animals, inspiring nail polish

shades, wardrobe pieces, soundtracks—you get it. Keep going. Have fun with it. Then circle all of the things you have now in red, followed by all of the things you have access to now in green, and finally all of the things you could have access to this year in blue. You can keep going if you feel it, circling goals for three years to five years ahead in black.

3 Close your eyes and visualize yourself in the future when you have just reached your goal. Write about how you feel (using the present tense, not future tense). See if any anecdotes come up about the path you took to get here. Write for at least twenty minutes without stopping.

Repeat this process as often as you like, preferably weekly with different goals.

Sagittarius Season Tarot Spread

Gain insight into the influences on your goals so you can work with and navigate through them. Use this spread weekly during Sagittarius season and as needed throughout the year for guidance on which aspect of your goals to focus on.

Begin by choosing one of the Aces to represent the element most closely associated with your goal, then select the rest of the cards as you would any other tarot spread. You can do the spread multiple times with different Aces to gain insight into different aspects of the goal.

1 Your goal

2 Wisdom from your past supporting your goal

3 What you can do in the present to support your goal

4 Guidance on how to support your goal in the future

5 Influences from the past

6 Influences in the present

7 Influences in the future

Sample reading

The Ace of Swords was chosen to represent a writing goal. Your comfort with flexibility has been a great help. Step into your leadership role to guide the project and others will follow. Your natural gravity is becoming more and more apparent and will draw others to support you.

Conflicting opinions from the past have added up to cause anxiety in the present. When you feel your stress growing, take a step back and pause for some deep breaths. Remind yourself of your greater goal and your ability to see it to fruition. You are integrating new avenues of creativity and action that will continue to develop and replace the old.

Cards pulled

1 Ace of Swords

2 Four of Wands

3 The Emperor

4 Strength

5 Three of Swords

6 Five of Swords

7 Page of Wands

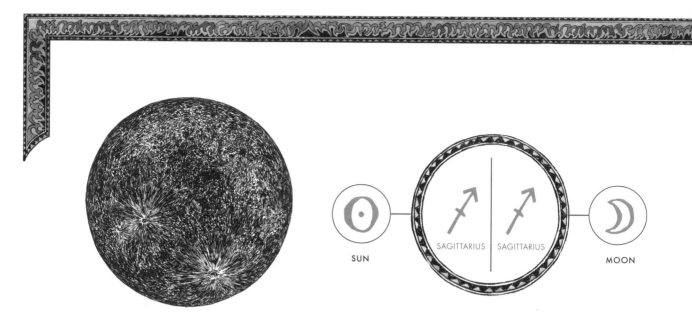

SUN — SAGITTARIUS | SAGITTARIUS — MOON

New Moon: Sun in Sagittarius, Moon in Sagittarius

The new moon in Sagittarius is our annual invitation to laugh in the face of adversity and see clearly the promise of tomorrow.

The fog is lifting and you can now see how clouded your vision has been. Embrace this new view and take a moment to drink it all in. Everyone has their own circumstances to work within, their own strengths and challenges. None of this determines the size of the dreams they are allowed to have or the amount of joy they can feel from living their life. You are ready and able, right now, to enjoy your life and be hopeful for the future.

The ritual for this new moon is designed to form a connection between your current and future selves, offering a way to share joy across time and space.

Temperance

The Wheel of Fortune

New Moon Ritual

Gather what you have of the following:

- Smoke, spray, or bell
- Printouts or drawings of Temperance and The Wheel of Fortune cards
- Pen
- Peridot or green aventurine
- Tea candle

1 Clear the energy of your space (see page 22), then close your eyes and take three deep, cleansing breaths to ground yourself.

2 On the back of the image of Temperance, write a note to your future self. Address yourself by name and write about one thing that is wonderful in your life right now.

3 On the back of the image of The Wheel of Fortune, write a note to your present self from your future self. Choose any time in the future. Address yourself by name and write about one thing that is wonderful in that future life.

4 Place the Temperance note image side down with The Wheel of Fortune image side up on top (the writing sides should be facing each other) and set the peridot or green aventurine on the very top.

5 Set a tea candle in front of the notes and light it. Let the candle burn all the way out (see page 23), then carry the crystal with you in your pocket for as long as you like as an amulet of luck.

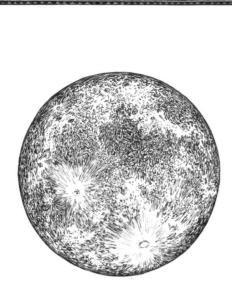

SUN | SAGITTARIUS | GEMINI | MOON

Full Moon: Sun in Sagittarius, Moon in Gemini

The full moon of Sagittarius season is in the opposite sign of Gemini. The full moon in Gemini is our annual opportunity to walk away from any patterns of language or interaction that are getting in the way of our long-term vision for the future.

The Sagittarius/Gemini axis makes sure we keep our words in line with our actions. It is easy to get the two disconnected. Language we've grown up using becomes outdated, patterns we pick up to make ourselves or others comfortable begin to backfire, or we simply haven't yet begun to describe ourselves in a manner appropriate for the person we are in the process of becoming. This full moon helps us recognize what we're ready to move on from and find the right words to express what we hope for.

The ritual for this full moon is designed to open new channels of expression in support of your development and to release limiting language impeding that development.

Full Moon Ritual

Gather what you have of the following:

- Smoke, spray, or bell
- Light blue seven-day ritual candle
- Printouts or drawings of the Temperance and Page of Swords cards
- Pen
- Moss agate and blue lace agate
- One sprig each of fresh parsley and mint

1 Clear the energy of your space (see page 22), then close your eyes and take three deep, cleansing breaths to ground yourself.

2 Place the candle in the center of your altar.

3 On the back of the Temperance image, write one main overarching goal you would like to channel your energy into. Write in the present tense, as if this is already your reality.

4 On the back of the Page of Swords image write:

"I am free of all language separating me from my goals. Supportive, encouraging language flows easily to and through me."

5 Read your goal from the Temperance card aloud, then set it image side up in front of the candle.

6 Read the incantation from the back of the Page of Swords aloud, then set it image side up on top of the Temperance image.

7 Place the crystals on top of the images.

8 Arrange the parsley and mint around the base of the candle.

9 Light the candle and spend a few minutes visualizing that you are breathing pale blue light into your throat and exhaling any stagnant energy.

10 Let the candle burn until it goes out on its own (see page 23).

CAPRICORN

CARDINAL

EARTH

Capricorn Season

DECEMBER 22–JANUARY 19 • CARDINAL EARTH • I EARN...

Capricorn is symbolized by the sea-goat, a hybrid creature with roots reaching back to ancient Mesopotamia. Goats are extremely agile climbers, not discouraged by terrain that other animals would never attempt. With the sea-goat, this agility takes to the water. This ability to tackle the most difficult terrain on land or sea makes Capricorn the great work inspiration of the zodiac.

The resources that are the least tangible are often the most valuable—time, energy, goodwill. In Capricorn season, while you navigate through the holidays, family obligations, and new year resolutions, make time to clear the haze of people pleasing and social contracts. The greatest gift you can give yourself is an accurate assessment of where your time and energy are being spent. You may find that you really do have the resources to pursue a goal you've been putting off when you make informed decisions about the allocation of your attention. In a culture that thrives on showing us what we don't have, choosing to see what you DO have is a radical act of self-love and support.

When you see clearly what you are working with, you can find the solid ground beneath your feet, get your bearings, and take meaningful steps toward your goals. Grounded, methodical

planning can feel limiting (see Capricorn in Tarot on page 126), but it actually opens up potential for play and exploration. Finding the floor and making plans based on current available resources frees you to narrow your focus, conserving time and energy, and leaving space for expansion when and if more resources become available. Most often, when we do the work of meticulously accounting for what we have, we find there is more there than we thought, especially when we make the cuts and plug the leaks that have gone neglected for too long.

Taking practical steps toward achievable goals is the bedrock of a magickal life. Working smarter, not harder, knowing when to rest and restore, making the most of the resources at hand, seeing opportunities in challenges that arise. We are all starting from somewhere and

Capricorn season is a time to focus your effort on what you would like to work toward in the year ahead.

wherever we are, we have exactly what we need to get to the next step. There are no shortcuts. There is only perseverance. Take the time now to assess what you can accomplish over the next year within your current circumstances. The universe is watching. The Divine is listening. Most importantly, YOU are witnessing your own accomplishment, earning your own respect and admiration, opening your vision to bigger and more challenging dreams and goals.

The Sun moves through Capricorn just after the winter solstice in the Northern Hemisphere and just after the summer solstice in the Southern Hemisphere (see page 11), one of the two points in the year when day and night are most disparate in length. While the Sun travels through Capricorn, use mundane means to produce magickal results.

Capricorn in Tarot

The sign of Capricorn is associated with The Devil card—not generally considered a welcome visitor of the deck, but a carrier of extremely valuable guidance. The Devil challenges us to tap into the most Capricorn part of ourselves, the most tenacious, unyielding, unsentimental depth, and get to work freeing ourselves from perceived limits. Untying the oppressive cords that bind us, that we bind ourselves with, takes more than a shift in mindset, more than a surrender to release. It takes work, pure and simple. The Capricorn sun is here to inspire and support that work.

Capricorn is ruled by Saturn, planet of contraction, associated with The World. If you had any doubt about the importance of breaking free, look to the transformative power of The World and its promise of the completion of a cycle and fresh start of another for inspiration.

The Devil

The World

Capricorn Season Activities

- Making a budget
- Organizing your office
- Taking your vitamins
- Trying out a new exercise plan
- Saying no to party invitations
- Saying yes to business lunches
- Shopping for antiques
- Opening a savings account
- Playing chess
- Plotting out your path to maximum productivity
- Ruthless devotion to your most meaningful work

Capricorn Season Journaling

The practical nature of Capricorn energy demands grounded exploration of your life and everything in it. Leave the big crazy dreams and aspirational visions for other seasons. Instead, just like Santa Claus in the song announcing his imminent arrival, focus on making a list and checking it twice.

Begin by making lists of everything you can think of (bonus points for ranked lists): places you've lived, vacation spots, home decor styles, pet names, favorite songs, best concert memories, capital cities, world languages, Oscar winners, pop stars. Do this until you have ten lists of ten.

Next, turn your gaze inward and begin making lists of your accomplishments. Every time you've set a goal and achieved it—and every time you pushed yourself harder, every time you thought you couldn't and proved yourself wrong. Think of every single award you've ever earned, from the attendance award in grade school to the most prestigious professional awards. Gather up all your awards of recognition in list form. Remind yourself what you are capable of.

Now you are ready for your final set of lists: your lists of goals. Look back to your vision lists from Sagittarius season. Choose one vision from each area of life and list the next three steps you can take in this month and in the next year toward reaching that goal.

Capricorn Season Tarot Spread

This spread is designed to help you break through obstacles and find your personal path of greatest return.

In the first level of meaning, the cards trace the narrative of the work you are focusing on (in order, 1–9) and show what you are invited to focus on and overcome on your way to earning great rewards.

In the second level of meaning, the columns provide insight on your motivating factors (left column), your inner transformation (center column), and who you become through this process (right column). For each of the columns, consider the center card the main message with the other two cards contributing to or supporting that message.

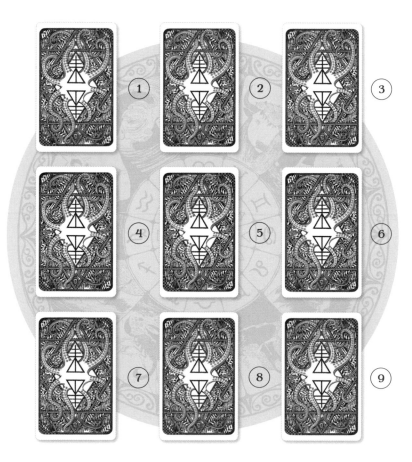

Sample reading

Your path ahead is challenging, but incredibly rewarding. Letting go, finding passion, great insight leading to a major breakdown to breakthrough, and finally an emotional journey to great love and abundance.

Give each of these stops on the way the time and attention they deserve.

Your desire to break free and start fresh is taking you through lessons on how big and powerful your heart truly is. Give yourself the gift of a free and hopeful heart. You are becoming a beacon of love.

Do not be discouraged by difficulties along the way. They, too, are there to help.

Cards pulled

1 Death

2 Knight of Coins

3 Ace of Swords

4 The Tower

5 Seven of Cups

6 Six of Cups

7 Ace of Cups

8 Queen of Cups

9 The Empress

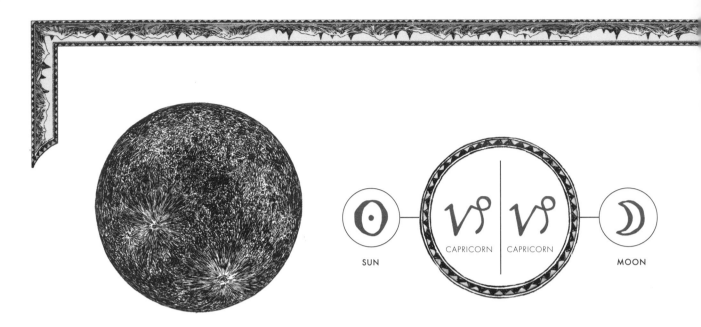

SUN · CAPRICORN | CAPRICORN · MOON

New Moon: Sun in Capricorn, Moon in Capricorn

The new moon in Capricorn is our annual invitation to establish habits of work that will lead us steadily toward realizing our goals. Getting started on the right foot means first making sure the path is clear. What have you been keeping yourself from? What goal, ideal, or identity do you tell yourself is just not in the cards for you this time around? How have you integrated the limiting beliefs of other individuals or collectives as your own? Are you ready to free yourself from these beliefs? Yes. The answer is yes. You got this. Go get 'em, sea goat!

The ritual for this new moon is designed to help you establish a new focused era of grounded practicality, determination, and discipline.

XXI

The World

New Moon Ritual

Gather what you have of the following:

- Smoke, spray, or bell
- Citrine and quartz crystal
- Printout or drawing of The World card
- Pen
- String or twine
- Seven tea candles
- Scissors

1 Clear the energy of your space (see page 22).

2 Holding the citrine in your left hand and quartz crystal in your right hand, close your eyes and take three deep, cleansing breaths to ground yourself.

3 On the back of The World image, write three statements describing your ideal life/work/ daily routine. For example,

"I make progress toward my goals every day"

or

"My physical and mental health support and are supported by my work."

4 Fold the image of The World (image side out) three times, tie it up with string, and place it in the center of your altar.

5 Set one candle directly in front of the World image bundle and place the crystals on either side of it.

6 Light a candle every day for seven days. Let each candle burn until it goes out on its own (see page 23).

7 On the seventh day, cut the string from the image of The World, open it, and read what you wrote aloud.

8 Keep the paper in your wallet or workspace until the next Capricorn season.

SUN   CAPRICORN | CANCER   MOON

Full Moon: Sun in Capricorn, Moon in Cancer

The full moon of Capricorn season is in the opposite sign of Cancer. The full moon in Cancer is our annual opportunity to brighten our hearts by prioritizing connection and disengaging from drama.

The Capricorn/Cancer axis explores the spectrum of practicality and emotionality, the drive to work versus the need to nurture. The sea goat pulls our minds to the surface, but the attention of our hearts remains in the depths, on the seafloor with the crab. Any emotional issues that need tending are lit up by this moon. Watch for clues from loved ones that their needs are not being met as well as they could be and check in with your own. How have your relationships grown and evolved? Have any of them fallen or drifted apart? What did those experiences teach you about what you value in yourself and others?

The ritual for this full moon is designed to open your heart and clear any obstacles to putting in the work to deepen the relationships you cherish the most.

Full Moon Ritual

Gather what you have of the following:

- Smoke, spray, or bell
- Printouts or drawings of The Devil and Two of Cups cards
- Pen
- Salt
- Small dish of water
- Rose quartz and black tourmaline
- Rose oil

1 Clear the energy of your space (see page 22), then close your eyes and take three deep, cleansing breaths to ground yourself.

2 Keep your eyes closed and observe your breath, as you visualize breathing in soft pink light on your inhale, breathing it in until it fills your entire body. On your exhale, blow out any stagnant energy around your heart. If there is a symbol attached to it for you or a particular memory or name, visualize that being released from your body as well. Do this for nine breath cycles, then gently open your eyes.

3 On the back of the image of The Devil, write down anything you can name that was released with your breath, then set the paper in the center of your altar, image side down.

4 Sprinkle salt on top of the paper.

5 Place the Two of Cups image side up, crossing The Devil.

6 Set the dish of water on top of the Two of Cups along with the crystals.

7 Add a few drops of rose oil to the water and then anoint yourself by touching a drop to your heart.

8 Let the spell sit under the full moon for one full night, then dispose of the water and paper. Rip the image of The Devil into pieces before disposing. If you like, keep the Two of Cups image as a reminder of your work.

Aquarius Season

JANUARY 20–FEBRUARY 18 • FIXED AIR • I BELIEVE...

Aquarius is symbolized by the water bearer, keeper of the sacred essence of life on Earth. The water bearer is traditionally depicted pouring the water out of a large vessel, a personified version of the flow of fresh water that makes life possible. Much of this water flows in annual cycles, arriving at the same time each year in floods or swells, creating a sense of trust and hope that the world will provide, will care for life, year after year.

We think of individuality as a quality that separates a person from a group, and that's true in a sense. Expressing what makes you unique by definition displays differences from others. But seeing these differences can actually bring us closer together as people. Compassionate individuality celebrates what is distinctive and complementary about us in relation to others. It creates an environment that values diversity and collective success over valorizing the rugged loner. Compassionate individuality shatters the bootstrap myth and exposes the truth that no one exists in a vacuum. We all shine brighter when we take turns focusing our lights on the eccentricities that make our individual personalities and contributions special, in loving symbiosis.

When we trust that others will care for us as we care for them, we generate hope. Hoping is not the same as wishing. Wishing invests energy on a specific outcome or object of desire.

Hoping is the repeated act of choosing to leave the door open for benevolence to come in. While being hopeful is sometimes an innate trait of a person, most often it is achieved through practice. When your mind fixates on possible negative outcomes of a stressful situation, remind yourself of all the equally plausible positive outcomes. The unknown is not inherently scary. The fantastical is not inherently impossible. In all the thousands of years of humans, in all the big wide world, you are right here, right now, reading this book. That is amazing to me! It makes me believe anything is possible. That is hope—the acceptance of wild and amazing possibilities.

When hope becomes focused, we find our ideals. It is wonderful to know yourself more deeply by shining a light on what you want to see more of in the world. The trick is, once you do, you've got to do something about it.

Aquarius season is a time to form a vision of your ideal world and find your role in creating it.

Ungrounded idealism quickly fades into detached fantasy, leaving you disappointed and disillusioned. Finding one thing you can do to bring that idealized world into existence keeps the channel of hope open and allows you to continue to refine your vision of yourself and your future and sets an example of idealism that is far from unrealistic. Your example can inspire others to follow what they believe in and to focus their own vision of the world to aspire to, each unique individual contributing to the greater good.

While the Sun travels through Aquarius, discover the unique beacon of hope you offer to the world.

Aquarius in Tarot

Aquarius is associated with The Star. The eight-pointed star is the version of the shape that graces most traditional decks. It is the star of the goddess Ishtar, of Venus, of the great universal creator. The Star reminds us that we exist in an ancient unbroken lineage of divine, nurturing, creative, receptive forces, that we are the ones we have been waiting for. It is a call to action and a call to peace. The unapologetic hope of The Star is the opposite of naive. It is woven into the fabric of time and space.

Aquarius' ruling planet, Uranus, is associated with The Fool, grounding this ancient wisdom in the present moment and reminding us to trust in the process, here and now.

The Star

The Fool

Aquarius Season Activities

- Making your own clothes or jewelry

- Trying a vegetable-based diet

- Reading biographies of visionary leaders

- Imagining your ideal world

- Radical acts of kindness

- Dancing with strangers

- Supporting a humanitarian cause

- Leaning in to your eccentricities

- Listening to the original Broadway cast recording of Hair

- Standing up for peace

Aquarius Season Journaling

Exploring your belief system through writing can be very revealing and extremely valuable. Here are four aspects to investigate this season.

Week One: What you believe is true.

Every day, write about at least one thing you believe is true. This can be one sentence or a list of things. Think broadly, from the micro to the macro. At least once during the week, spend 15–20 minutes writing about why you believe something is true. Does your reasoning hold up?

Week Two: What you believe about your past.

What is the story you tell about your past? What beliefs are embedded in this story and how do they affect how you see yourself and your place in the world? Is there anything that you would like to tell differently upon reflection? Cycle through these questions throughout the week, writing a few pages every day.

Week Three: What you believe you are capable of.

Now that you've examined how you got here, take a close look into what you believe you are capable of. What is your superpower? Your weakness? How do you work around your weakness or balance it with your superpower? What could you accomplish if you set your mind to it—today? This year?

Week Four: What you believe is possible.

Read back through everything you've written over the past three weeks. What common themes emerge? Are there clues? Is there an ideal world taking shape? How can you bring that possibility closer to reality? Find the limit of what you believe is possible, then push yourself to expand that vision of the future.

Aquarius Season Tarot Spread

Explore the root of your beliefs and how to effectively bring them to life in the world. This is a great spread to do for each of your core beliefs and ideals. Make notes for each and look for similarities and differences in the spreads. These readings as a whole can give you another layer of information about common themes that inspire and motivate you. If you want to repeat the spread for the same belief, wait at least two weeks between readings.

1 The belief or ideal in question—choose a card from the deck that most closely represents this, then pull the rest of the cards as you would for any other reading.

2 Your role in amplifying this belief

3 A skill that can help you more effectively work for this belief

4 A quality to look for in others who can help you

5 Another way to look at this belief

Sample reading

The Three of Coins was chosen to represent desire for collaboration in work. If you want to work with others, you've got to come out and say it. Communication is the key to attracting suitable collaborators. Trust your voice. You know exactly what to say. Try looking at things from different perspectives. See yourself how your best friend sees you. Imagine your project from another angle—the more viewpoints, the better.

You need to be surrounded by people who can articulate their emotions. Listen for nuance and depth in conversations. The collaboration you seek is not only practical, it is also in the service of a larger loving community.

Cards pulled

1 Three of Coins

2 Ten of Swords

3 The Hanged Man

4 Queen of Swords

5 Ten of Cups

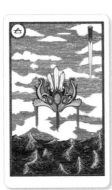

The Hanged Man

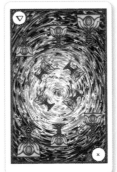

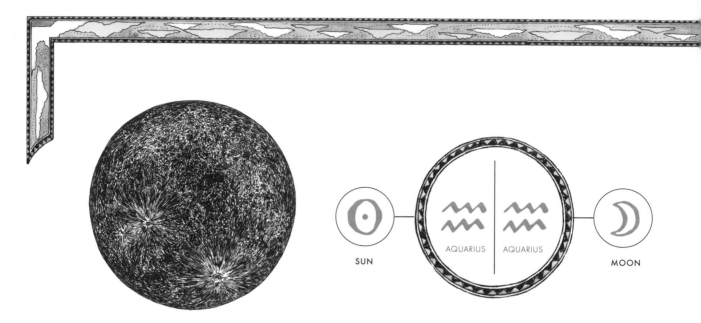

New Moon: Sun in Aquarius, Moon in Aquarius

The new moon in Aquarius is our annual invitation to reaffirm our commitment to our ideals and our collective humanity.

Gorgeous Aquarian energy—independent, idealistic, compassionate—is here to shower us with uncompromising hope, rooted in a deep, inner knowing that the world can be a place that truly sustains and nurtures all. It is easy to focus on what needs to be changed instead of the change itself, to get dragged down by the relentless horrors we see and hear about every day. It is time to shift that focus. When you choose to be unapologetically hopeful and driven to be a living example of an ideal world, you light up like a beacon in the night, calling others to do so as well, announcing it is safe.

The ritual for this new moon is designed to open your perception to see the foundation of your ideal world already in place in the material plane and to fuel your imagination and your will to continue to bring it into full existence.

The Star

New Moon Ritual

Gather what you have of the following:

- Smoke, spray, or bell
- Small nail
- White taper candle
- Candle holder or small plate
- Printout or drawing of The Star card
- Honey in a small dish
- Chrysocolla
- Incense (preferably sandalwood)

1 Clear the energy of your space (see page 22), then close your eyes and take three deep, cleansing breaths to ground yourself.

2 Using the small nail, carve the words "I shine as a beacon of the expanse of the possible" into the surface of the candle.

3 Place the candle in the candle holder or melt the bottom a little and stick it to the plate.

4 Set the image of The Star in front of the candle, then set the dish of honey in the center of it and the chrysocolla in front of the dish.

5 Light the incense, then gently close your eyes. Spend a few minutes envisioning the world you want to live in, the quality of life you desire for your community, for all of humanity. Let the picture get very rich and vibrant in your mind, then open your eyes.

6 Light the candle and say the words,

"It is so."

7 Let the candle burn until it goes out on its own (see page 23). When it is done, discard the wax, honey, and paper. Keep the chrysocolla with you at all times for one week.

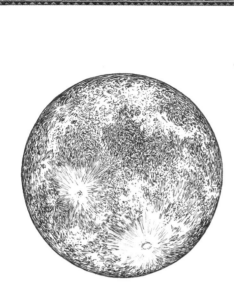

SUN · AQUARIUS | LEO · MOON

Full Moon: Sun in Aquarius, Moon in Leo

The full moon of Aquarius season is in the opposite sign of Leo. The full moon in Leo is our annual opportunity to learn how to shine for ourselves by shining for all.

The Aquarius/Leo axis is the axis of the collective and the individual self, the need to evolve the collective and the desire to stand out from the crowd. Under this Leo moon, the lion's grandiosity takes an altruistic turn as the water bearer casts a soothing spell on the savage beast. Any points of pride getting in the way of deep soul connection with the group are washed away and replaced with curiosity and understanding. Where do you see the separation between yourself and others most clearly? What similarities can you find there that force that line to blur?

The ritual for this full moon is designed to shine the light of truth on the unique parts of you that connect you most strongly to the collective.

Full Moon Ritual

Gather what you have of the following:

- **Smoke, spray, or bell**
- **Printouts or drawings of Strength and the Ace of Swords cards**
- **Three tea candles**
- **Rhodochrosite and citrine**

1 Clear the energy of your space (see page 22), then close your eyes and take three deep, cleansing breaths to ground yourself.

2 Place the Strength image on the left side of your altar and the Ace of Swords on the right.

3 Set one tea candle on each image and one in the middle in front (closest to you).

4 Place the crystals beside the middle candle, with the rhodochrosite on the left and the citrine on the right.

5 Light the candle on the Strength image, then the candle on the Ace of Swords, followed by the central candle.

6 Close your eyes and visualize a flame burning within your chest. Using your breath, grow the light of the flame until it envelops your body, the room, your neighborhood, the world. Then gently open your eyes and see if you can still feel that connection.

7 Let the candles burn until they go out on their own (see page 23).

AQUARIUS SEASON

PISCES

Pisces Season

FEBRUARY 19-MARCH 20 • MUTABLE WATER • I DREAM...

MUTABLE

▽

WATER

Pisces is symbolized by the fish. We live on the same planet as the fish but in a completely different world, requiring vastly different physiology. In contemplating the wonder of two such disparate worlds existing on the same planet, our consciousness can begin to expand, accepting the possibility of other, less visible worlds floating in our sphere of existence and the hidden complexity of the substance we move through every day.

There is a current running through everything, like the water in our bodies, in the air, in the soil. It can remain undetectable for decades, even generations, to all but a few who choose to see it. Artists may call it being visited by the muse, the religious moved by the spirit, but there are more subtle manifestations as well. You get an uncomfortable, eerie feeling and stop abruptly at the curb moments before a car races though the red light, or recall a memory related to a song just before it starts to play on the radio. You meet someone you connect with immediately and feel like you've known them forever. Maybe you have. We are connected to each other and the world around us in wonderful and mysterious ways. Take a break from trying to understand why or how and accept this universal fabric as one more layer of reality.

Existing in this energetic web of interconnectedness means that things that affect others can also affect you. When you feel this, it's called empathy. Sometimes empathy can be misunderstood or misidentified. It can be confusing to feel emotions that do not seem related to your own experience. Instead of trying to push those feelings away or ignore them, try giving yourself a little time and space to invite them in, to listen to what they have to tell you. Empathy can increase your understanding of your loved ones, of colleagues and collaborators, and of groups of people in your community and the world. When you recognize and embrace your empathic powers, you can not only appreciate the experiences of others more fully, but you can also allow these feelings that do not belong to you to pass through you, leaving understanding

Pisces season is a time to tap into the unseen world flowing all around you.

and taking their energetic weight away with them. You may feel what others feel deeply, but only keep what is your own.

There is a whole other world we are also connected to that exists in parallel to our material world and is perfect for exploring this season—the dream world. Have you ever had a dream that felt so real that even after you woke up, the emotions of the dream stayed with you for the rest of the day? What would it be like to accept that the world of dreams is real, another reality that functions in a different way? Dreams bring us valuable messages and insights. They can help you understand yourself and your life in ways that intellectual analysis cannot. The language of dreams combines personal and universally significant symbols to unveil the guidance, wisdom, and meaning weaving their way through the mythology of your life.

While the Sun travels through Pisces, get fluent in the language of your own mystical journey.

Pisces in Tarot

Pisces is associated with The Moon—reflective, introspective, intuitive, mysterious. The Moon brightens the dark corners of our minds, exposing those fears and secrets that can finally be faced and dealt with. When we face our shadows, we are shown exactly what we need to grow in the present moment. Understanding the mysteries hidden within unlocks the unique magick we have formed during our lives.

Pisces' ruling planet, Neptune, is associated with The Hanged Man, teaching us to seek out and expect radical shifts in perspective as we embark on the journey within.

The Moon

The Hanged Man

Pisces Season Activities

- Taking an art class

- Stargazing

- Adopting an animal into your home or virtually through a wildlife organization

- Crystal shopping

- Floating in a sensory deprivation tank

- Making psychic connections

- Night swimming

- Attending a concert—or giving one

- Daydreaming

- Being a sympathetic ear

Pisces Season Journaling

Prepare to get cozy with your unconscious mind with a dream journal. Keeping a dream journal is as simple as having a notebook and pen at your bedside so you can easily record your dreams immediately when you wake up, before they begin to fade. It is a wonderful way to track messages from your subconscious and find what images and themes recur for you, forming your personal symbolic language. You can use your main journal for this or, if you really get into it, you may choose to keep a dedicated notebook just for dreams.

When you record your dreams, do so as soon as you wake up and include as much detail as possible. Do not try to interpret as you go. Just get the information down on paper. You are acting as a journalist investigating your own subconscious. Accuracy and immediacy in gathering information are your best friends.

You don't need complete sentences or even coherent ideas. Stream-of-consciousness lists of words, colors, images, or feelings are great— write whatever you can capture. After you've noted all you can, put the journal away. Do not read back through it. The temptation to begin interpreting will be too great.

At the end of the week, read back through your entries to see what meaning forms for you. Are there obvious connections to situations in your waking life? New ways of understanding the past? Clues about what you truly want to move toward in the future? If so, great! If not, that's fine too. Sometimes it takes a long time for the meaning in symbolic messages to become clear. Be patient and keep going.

Pisces Season Tarot Spread

We all have gifts that are useful and valuable to ourselves and others, but it can be hard to see what they are or to identify which gift is most appropriate in a given situation. This spread helps you see your unique abilities by getting you in touch with your secret superpower.

Which of our powers are most beneficial shifts depending on the time and circumstances. You can use this spread to gain insight into your power overall, in a certain area of life, or in a specific situation.

1 The realm and general nature of your secret superpower

2 First step to developing this superpower

3 What strengthens the superpower

4 What weakens the superpower

5 How you can best use this power for good

6 Seen effect on the world

7 Unseen effect on the world

Sample reading

You have a profound natural ability to make others feel calm and help them identify what gets in the way of that calm. Start to put some structure around it. Notice what you say, how you signal you are listening, your general body language, everything that comes along with this power. Remain hopeful and do not try to reinvent the wheel. What you are doing naturally is great. Where you want to take this gift is entirely up to you. Wave your wand and make it happen! Your power gives others permission to set boundaries around their sacred space and gives you a new understanding of your values.

Cards pulled

1 Four of Cups

2 Two of Coins

3 The Star

4 Page of Cups

5 Ace of Wands

6 The High Priestess

7 Four of Swords

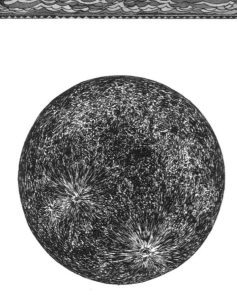

SUN   PISCES   PISCES   MOON

New Moon: Sun in Pisces, Moon in Pisces

The new moon in Pisces is our annual invitation to dive deep into our psyches to retrieve and activate the magick that has been lying dormant, waiting patiently to come to the surface.

Psychic downloads, seas of empathy and compassion, and good old-fashioned cosmic weirdness conspire to draw your attention to your magickal abilities. What do your friends come to you for? Are you able to see the solution to a problem? Do you have an amazing knack for knowing exactly how someone needs to be comforted? An eerily accurate ability to navigate around traffic? Do animals gravitate to you? Identifying your gifts is the first step in developing them to their full potential.

The ritual for this new moon is designed to reveal the innate gift that is most valuable to you at this time and to help you see how well equipped you are to work with it.

The Moon

New Moon Ritual

Gather what you have of the following:

- **Smoke, spray, or bell**
- **Purple seven-day ritual candle**
- **Labradorite**
- **Printout or drawing of The Moon card**
- **Pen**
- **Three cinnamon sticks**

1 Clear the energy of your space (see page 22), then close your eyes and take three deep, cleansing breaths to ground yourself.

2 Place the candle in the center of your altar area and light it.

3 Take the labradorite in your hands and hold it against your body, just under your diaphragm.

4 Gently close your eyes and envision yourself deep in an underwater cave. The temperature is comfortable and you can breathe just fine. It is so deep that there is no light at all, but you can feel yourself transforming, mystical powers making their way to the surface of your being. A glowing fish swims by and illuminates a large mirror just a few feet in front of you. You see yourself reflected for the first time and you notice there is something different about you. What is it?

5 Open your eyes and write down the power that was revealed to you on the back of The Moon image, then fold it in half and place it in front of the candle.

6 Set the labradorite on top of the folded paper, then arrange the cinnamon sticks in a triangle around it, pointing toward the candle.

7 Let the candle burn until it goes out on its own (see page 23), then place the cinnamon sticks in a small pan with 3 cups (720 ml) of water. Bring to a boil, then cover and simmer for ten minutes. Let cool, strain, then drink the cinnamon tea. Keep the labradorite as a talisman of your magick, and discard the paper after you've noted what you wrote in your journal with your ritual notes.

PISCES SEASON

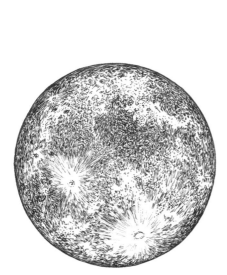

SUN   PISCES | VIRGO   MOON

Full Moon: Sun in Pisces, Moon in Virgo

The full moon of Pisces season is in the opposite sign of Virgo. The full moon in Virgo is our annual opportunity to polish up the reflection of our belief system and spiritual goals in our daily rituals.

The Pisces/Virgo axis explores the spectrum of spiritual practices, from the esoteric and transcendental to the practical devotion of daily rituals. Everything we do—*everything*—is a manifestation of our value system: the food we eat, where we get it, and how it's grown; the clothes we wear and where they come from; the work we are drawn to and how much of ourselves we give to it. Whether we are conscious of it or not, every choice we make informs us and others about what we deem important in the world. The exterior markers we gather around ourselves act as a mirror of our inner aspirations.

The ritual for this full moon is designed to reflect back to you what your material world says about your spiritual values and gently loosen any that send an inaccurate message.

Full Moon Ritual

Gather what you have of the following:

- Smoke, spray, or bell
- Printouts or drawings of The Hermit and The Moon cards
- Dark blue seven-day ritual candle
- Four small sticks, preferably from a tree near your home
- Lapis lazuli and four small black tourmaline crystals

1 Clear the energy of your space (see page 22), then close your eyes and take three deep, cleansing breaths to ground yourself.

2 Set the images of The Hermit and The Moon next to each other so they are touching, with The Moon on the left and The Hermit on the right.

3 Place the candle on top of the images in the center, then make a square around the candle with the sticks.

4 Within the square, put one black tourmaline in each corner and the lapis lazuli in front of the candle.

5 Light the candle, then close your eyes. Spend a few minutes finding the most complete stillness you can, then visualize yourself alone in a temple. It is perfectly calm and peaceful,

charged with spiritual growth and divine connection. Notice what is similar to your own home about this place and what is different. Write down what you saw in your journal with your ritual notes.

6 Let the candle burn until it goes out on its own (see page 23). While it is burning, remove one item from your space each day that is not worthy of existing in your temple. This can be as simple as taking out the garbage or as complex as parting with a once-meaningful object you no longer connect with.

7 When the candle has burned all the way out, discard the sticks. Rinse the black tourmaline crystals under running water, then place one piece in each corner of your temple. Leave them in place until the next full moon.

Key Dates

The following charts give the dates of the new and full moons for the next few years. All times are UT (Universal Time). Keep in mind that your local date may be different depending on your time difference from UT.

Year: 2022–2023

	NEW MOON		FULL MOON	
Aries Season	Apr 1 | 06:24		Apr 16 | 18:55	
Taurus Season	Apr 30 | 20:28	*Partial solar eclipse*	May 16 | 04:14	*Total lunar eclipse*
Gemini Season	May 30 | 11:30		Jun 14 | 11:52	
Cancer Season	Jun 29 | 02:52		Jul 13 | 18:38	
Leo Season	Jul 28 | 17:55		Aug 12 | 01:36	
Virgo Season	Aug 27 | 08:17		Sep 10 | 09:59	
Libra Season	Sep 25 | 21:55		Oct 9 | 20:55	
Scorpio Season	Oct 25 | 10:49	*Partial solar eclipse*	Nov 8 | 11:02	*Total lunar eclipse*
Sagittarius Season	Nov 23 | 22:57		Dec 8 | 04:08	
Capricorn Season	Dec 23 | 10:17		Jan 6 | 23:08	
Aquarius Season	Jan 21 | 20:53		Feb 5 | 18:29	
Pisces Season	Feb 20 | 07:06		Mar 7 | 12:40	

Year: 2023–2024

	NEW MOON		FULL MOON	
Aries Season	Mar 21 | 17:23,		Apr 6 | 04:34	
	Apr 20 | 04:13	*Total solar eclipse*		
Taurus Season	May 19 | 15:53		May 5 | 17:34	*Penumbral lunar eclipse*
Gemini Season	Jun 18 | 04:37		Jun 4 | 03:42	
Cancer Season	Jul 17 | 18:32		Jul 3 | 11:39	
Leo Season	Aug 16 | 09:38		Aug 1 | 18:32	
Virgo Season	Sep 15 | 01:40		Aug 31 | 01:36	
Libra Season	Oct 14 | 17:55	*Annular solar eclipse*	Sep 29 | 09:58	
Scorpio Season	Nov 13 | 09:27		Oct 28 | 20:24	*Partial lunar eclipse*
Sagittarius Season	Dec 12 | 23:32		Nov 27 | 09:16	
Capricorn Season	Jan 11 | 11:57		Dec 27 | 00:33	
Aquarius Season	Feb 9 | 22:59		Jan 25 | 17:54	
Pisces Season	Mar 10 | 09:00		Feb 24 | 12:30	

Note: An annular solar eclipse is when the apparent size of the Moon is slightly smaller than that of the Sun, creating a "ring of fire" effect; a penumbral lunar eclipse is when the Moon is eclipsed only by the outer shadow (the penumbra) of the Earth, making a much more subtle eclipse.

Year: 2024–2025

	NEW MOON	FULL MOON
Aries Season	Apr 8 | 18:21 *Total solar eclipse*	Mar 25 | 07:00 *Penumbral lunar eclipse*
Taurus Season	May 8 | 03:22	Apr 23 | 23:49
Gemini Season	Jun 6 | 12:38	May 23 | 13:53
Cancer Season	Jul 5 | 22:57	Jun 22 | 01:08, Jul 21 | 10.17
Leo Season	Aug 4 | 11:13	Aug 19 | 18:26
Virgo Season	Sep 3 | 01:56	Sep 18 | 02:34 *Partial lunar eclipse*
Libra Season	Oct 2 | 18:49 *Annular solar eclipse*	Oct 17 | 11:26
Scorpio Season	Nov 1 | 12:47	Nov 15 | 21:28
Sagittarius Season	Dec 1 | 06:21	Dec 15 | 09:02
Capricorn Season	Dec 30 | 22:27	Jan 13 | 22:27
Aquarius Season	Jan 29 | 12:36	Feb 12 | 13:53
Pisces Season	Feb 28 | 00:45	Mar 14 | 06:55 *Total lunar eclipse*

Year: 2025–2026

	NEW MOON	FULL MOON
Aries Season	Mar 29 | 10:58 *Partial solar eclipse*	Apr 13 | 00:22
Taurus Season	Apr 27 | 19:31	May 12 | 16:56
Gemini Season	May 27 | 03:02	Jun 11 | 07:44
Cancer Season	Jun 25 | 10:32	Jul 10 | 20:37
Leo Season	Jul 24 | 19:11	Aug 9 | 07:55
Virgo Season	Aug 23 | 06:06, Sep 21 | 19:54 *Partial solar eclipse*	Sep 7 | 18:09 *Total lunar eclipse*
Libra Season	Oct 21 | 12:25	Oct 7 | 03:48
Scorpio Season	Nov 20 | 06:47	Nov 5 | 13:19
Sagittarius Season	Dec 20 | 01:43	Dec 4 | 23:14
Capricorn Season	Jan 18 | 19:52	Jan 3 | 10:03
Aquarius Season	Feb 17 | 12:01 *Annular solar eclipse*	Feb 1 | 22:09
Pisces Season	Mar 19 | 01:23	Mar 3 | 11:38 *Total lunar eclipse*

Year: 2026–2027

	🌑 NEW MOON	🌕 FULL MOON
Aries Season Taurus Season Gemini Season	Apr 17 | 11:52 May 16 | 20:01 Jun 15 | 02:54	Apr 2 | 02:12 May 1 | 17:23 May 31 | 08:45
Cancer Season Leo Season Virgo Season	Jul 14 | 09:44 Aug 12 | 17:37 *Total solar eclipse* Sep 11 | 03:27	Jun 29 | 23:57 Jul 29 | 14:36 Aug 28 | 04:18 *Partial lunar eclipse*
Libra Season Scorpio Season Sagittarius Season	Oct 10 | 15:50 Nov 9 | 07:02 Dec 9 | 00:52	Sep 26 | 16:49 Oct 26 | 04:12 Nov 24 | 14:53
Capricorn Season Aquarius Season Pisces Season	Jan 7 | 20:24 Feb 6 | 15:56 *Annular solar eclipse* Mar 8 | 09:29	Dec 24 | 01:28 Jan 22 | 12:17 Feb 20 | 23:24 *Penumbral lunar eclipse*

Year: 2027–2028

	🌑 NEW MOON	🌕 FULL MOON
Aries Season Taurus Season Gemini Season	Apr 6 | 23:51 May 6 | 10:59 Jun 4 | 19:40	Mar 22 | 10:44 Apr 20 | 22:27, May 20 | 10:59 Jun 19 | 00:44
Cancer Season Leo Season Virgo Season	Jul 4 | 03:02 Aug 2 | 10:05 *Total solar eclipse* Aug 31 | 17:41	Jul 18 | 15:45 *Penumbral lunar eclipse* Aug 17 | 07:29 *Penumbral lunar eclipse* Sep 15 | 23:03
Libra Season Scorpio Season Sagittarius Season	Sep 30 | 02:36 Oct 29 | 13:37 Nov 28 | 03:24	Oct 15 | 13:47 Nov 14 | 03:26 Dec 13 | 16:09
Capricorn Season Aquarius Season Pisces Season	Dec 27 | 20:12 Jan 26 | 15:12 *Annular solar eclipse* Feb 25 | 10:37	Jan 12 | 04:03 *Partial lunar eclipse* Feb 10 | 15:04 Mar 11 | 01:06

Year: 2028–2029

	● NEW MOON	● FULL MOON
Aries Season Taurus Season Gemini Season	Mar 26 | 04:31 Apr 24 | 19:47 May 24 | 08:16	Apr 9 | 10:27 May 8 | 19:49 Jun 7 | 06:09
Cancer Season Leo Season Virgo Season	Jun 22 | 18:27, Jul 22 | 03:02 *Total solar eclipse* Aug 20 | 10:44 Sep 18 | 18:24	Jul 6 | 18:11 *Partial lunar eclipse* Aug 5 | 08:10 Sep 3 | 23:48
Libra Season Scorpio Season Sagittarius Season	Oct 18 | 02:57 Nov 16 | 13:18 Dec 16 | 02:06	Oct 3 | 16:25 Nov 2 | 09:17 Dec 2 | 01:40
Capricorn Season Aquarius Season Pisces Season	Jan 14 | 17:24 *Partial solar eclipse* Feb 13 | 10:31 Mar 15 | 04:19	Dec 31 | 16:48 *Total lunar eclipse* Jan 30 | 06:04 Feb 28 | 17:10

Year: 2029–2030

	● NEW MOON	● FULL MOON
Aries Season Taurus Season Gemini Season	Apr 13 | 21:40 May 13 | 13:42 Jun 12 | 03:50 *Partial solar eclipse*	Mar 30 | 02:26 Apr 28 | 10:37 May 27 | 18:37
Cancer Season Leo Season Virgo Season	Jul 11 | 15:51 *Partial solar eclipse* Aug 10 | 01:56 Sep 8 | 10:44	Jun 26 | 03:22 *Total lunar eclipse* Jul 25 | 13:36 Aug 24 | 01:51, Sep 22 | 16:29
Libra Season Scorpio Season Sagittarius Season	Oct 7 | 19:14 Nov 6 | 04:24 Dec 5 | 14:52 *Partial solar eclipse*	Oct 22 | 09:28 Nov 21 | 04:03 Dec 20 | 22:46 *Total lunar eclipse*
Capricorn Season Aquarius Season Pisces Season	Jan 4 | 02:49 Feb 2 | 16:07 Mar 4 | 06:35	Jan 19 | 15:54 Feb 18 | 06:20 Mar 19 | 17:56

Index

Acknowledgments

Huge thanks once again to Rohan Daniel Eason for having an uncanny ability to turn my dreams and suggestions into gorgeous works of art. Your illustrations truly bring life to this book and joy to my heart. Carmel Edmonds, Sally Powell, Allan Sommerville, and everyone at CICO, thank you for the incredible work and care you poured into these pages. Cindy Richards, it's been such a pleasure working with you. Your trust in me and the projects we've done together are very greatly appreciated.

Anne Woodward, manager and confidante extraordinaire, your guidance and friendship are more precious than gold and twice as brilliant. I could not do this without you. My dearest Chris, your protection of me and my time and space made it possible for me to complete this work during an extremely difficult time. I love you. Thank you.

And deepest thanks to Jamie, for always seeing me even when I couldn't see myself. While I feel you with me still, your physical presence on Earth will forever be deeply missed. I'll see you again someday in the astral plane, on a frozen pond, gazing up at shooting stars. Until then, I'll carry your flame.

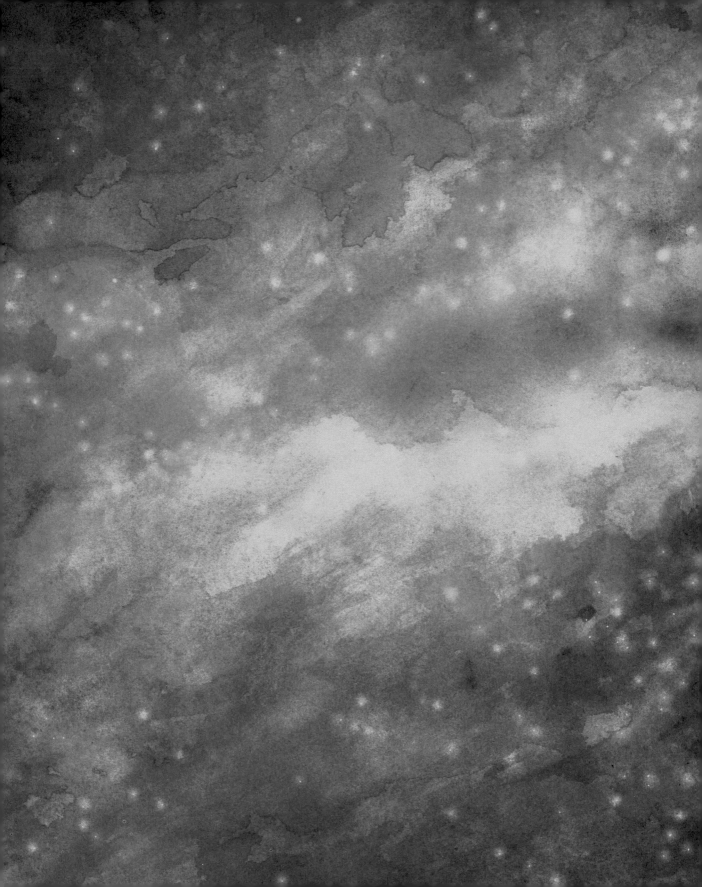